長谷良子リボンアート
リボンで花のクラフトワーク
YOSHIKO HASE'S RIBBON ART
監修・指導／長谷良子

◆この本をお買い上げ頂き誠にありがとうございました。手づくりの花をお作りになってお楽しみ下さい。（長谷良子）

■赤のチューリップ
Turip in Red
チェスキー・クルムロフの丘の上より、
遠くの風景に魅せられてひと休み。
材料 P61　型紙 P66

■ブラックカトリーヌ

Black Catherine
小雨煙るプラハ、カレル橋のたもとにて。
材料 P52　型紙 P70

■ミニカメリアローズ　■まじょのどくいちご
Mini-Camellia Rose/Majo-Majo Strawberry

古い町並みのカフェでドナウベンドの中央広場を背に
材料 P50・P57　型紙 P69・P76

■ブルーライトフラワー

Blue Light Flower

ハンガリーの古い石畳にたたずむオブジェに
花束を持たせて。
材料 P53　型紙 P72

■マルチカラーフラワー　■ベアグラス

Multi Color Flower/Beargrass

漁夫の砦より、ブダペストの町を花越しに眺めて。
材料 P52・P60　型紙 P70・P73

■ガーベラ
■キャロ君のばら
Gerbera/
Caro-Rose

エフェソスの生贄用の石の上に、とびきりの花を捧げて。
材料 P55　型紙 P72

■チューリップ　■パリのラナンキュラス

Turip/Ranunculus in Paris

ナイル川クルーズのティータイムに花を添えて。
材料 P55・P56　型紙 P73・P77

■まじょまじょのばら
■ライラック
■オーガンジースイートピー

**Majo-Majo Rose/Lilac/
Organdy Sweet pea**

ナイル川を眺めランチを楽しむテーブルアレンジメント。
材料 P54・P59・P60　型紙 P64・P72・P76

■ シルキーのユリ　　■ シルキーサンダーソニア

Lily/Silky-Sandersonia

遠くにバスタイ橋を眺めて、優しい風合いの花束を置いて。
材料 P59　型紙 P77・P79

■ ダリア

Dahlia

きらめくモハメット・アリのモスクの中、祈りの声を聞きながら。
材料 P61　型紙 P73

■ マルチカラーローズ
Multi color rose
夏の日差しを受け、リボンで華やかなバラを制作。
材料 P50　型紙 P69

■ フラワーマム

Flower Mum

古いコム・オンボの神殿に
溶け込む花。
材料 P62　型紙 P78

■ ホワイトローズ

White Rose

歴史物語の中に小さな花束を。
ホルス神殿の片隅に置いて
材料 P62　型紙 P78

■火の鳥　■ベアグラス

Fire Bird/Beargrass

アルシンベル巨大神殿に、私の情熱を赤い花にして。
材料 P49・P60　型紙 P67・P73

■まじょまじょのバラ　■まじょのどくいちご
Majo-Majo Rose/Majo-Majo Strawberry
ホルス神殿に照りつける太陽と赤バラに、黒のラッピングペーパーで力強さを表して。
材料 P50・P61　型紙 P64・P69

■キャベツ
　ローズ

Cabbage Rose

大きな花と大きな建造物と歴史の語らい。ハトシェプスト葬祭殿にて。

材料 P49　型紙 P67

■キャロ君の
　バラ

Caro-Rose

トルコ・セルケニク
考古学博物館で天体
の引力にひかれて。
材料 P55　型紙 P72

■ラッパ水仙
Daffodil
きらきらと光る水、パムツカレの石灰棚に軽やかな色彩の花束を置いて。
材料 P60　型紙 P78

■カトレア
■プルメリア
■シャネルオーキッド
Cattleya/Plumeria/Chanel Orchid
親しい人へのプレゼントに。ペーパーで作ったバッグの中にお気に入りの花をアレンジ。
材料 P58・P59　型紙 P77

■ガーベラ

Gerbera

一度は行ってみたいトルコ・カッパッドキアに花も一緒に連れて旅へ出た。
材料 P55　型紙 P74

■まじょの小花
Majo-small Flower
繊細な小花と、背景の自然
とのコントラストを表現。
材料 P62　型紙 P65

■まじょのグラジオラス

gladiolus

太陽をいっぱい浴びた花を、プールサイドで。
南国の夏の思い出。
材料 P63　型紙 P65

■ダイヤローズ

Diamond Rose

碧い海と太陽の夏の午後、バリにて。
材料 P53　型紙 P71

■サンバドロップ

Samba-Drop

ジョグジャカルタの遺跡、多くの信者の道に
祈りを捧げるように花かごを置いて。
材料 P51　型紙 P70

■ミステリーローズ
Mystery-Rose
バリの早朝グリーンの木々と
赤の花をバッグに入れて、胸
いっぱいの空気を吸って。
材料 P57　型紙 P79

■ぼたん
■めだかの葉っぱ

Peony/
Medaka leaf

中国、万里の長城に合わせてぼたんを創る

材料 P63　型紙 P75・P76

■春一番

First Spring Breeze

春霞を思わせる淡い色合いで、小花いっぱいのアレンジをテーブルに飾って。

材料 P52　型紙 P69

■ダイヤローズ
Diamond Rose
沈む太陽と個性あるシールの花、南国バリにて。
材料 P53　型紙 P71

■ローズホープ
Rose of Hope

午後のティータイムには
バラの花が一番。香港の
庭にて。
材料 P58　型紙 P74

■フリージア ■赤ちゃんの小枝 ■チューリップ ■オーガンジーのバラ ■マーガレット ■ライラック
Freesia/Baby Hand Branch/Tulip/Organdy-Rose/Farguerite/Lilac

私の作った花々を、全部一緒に可愛らしいカラーでまとめてアレンジ。
材料 P53・P54・P55　型紙 P70・P71・P73

■水色の涙
■まじょまじょのバラ
Blue Tears/Majo-Majo Rose

プールサイドにて、手作りのバッグにブルーの花々をアレンジして、リボンもブルーで。
材料 P49・P61　型紙 P64・P66

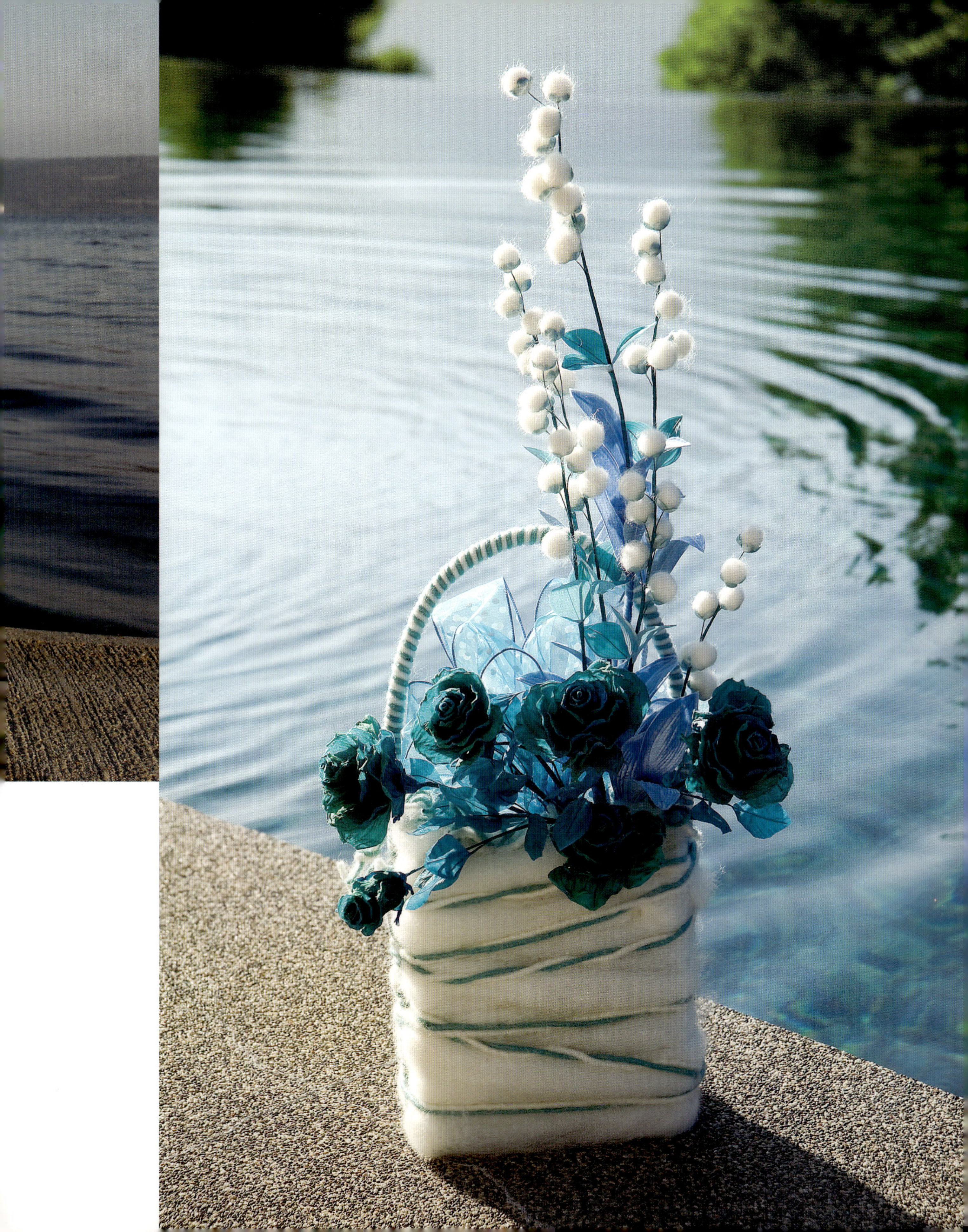

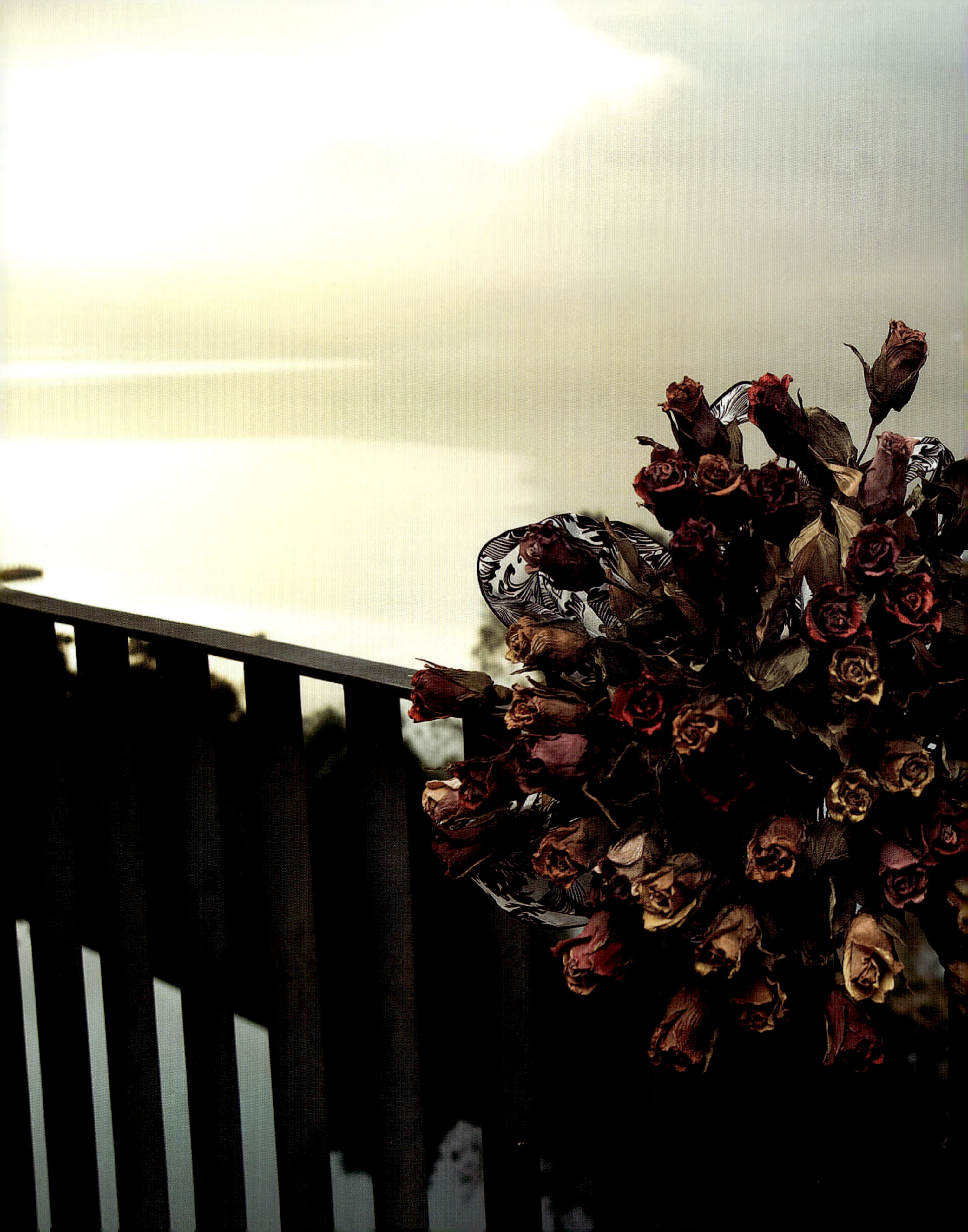

■日月潭

朝もやに煙る日月潭が幻想の世界へと。花と同化されて。
材料 P58　型紙 P74

■赤いカーネーショ
■まじょのどくいちご
Red-Carnation/
Majo-Majo Strawberry
個性的な赤いカーネーションを、いろいろな赤のリボン素材を取り合わせて制作。
材料 P50・P57　型紙 P69・P75

■なごみ
Nagomi
こんな表情の花束がプレゼントされたらいいな。
材料 P51　型紙 P67

■ 小さい菊の花
Small Daisy

淡い花柄のラッピングペーパーと花も淡い色でコーディネート。

材料 P48　型紙 P65

■ 風のアジサイ
Wind Hydrangea

春の風を思わせるような淡い色のアジサイを遺跡の上に飾り、遠い昔のことを考える。

材料 P48　型紙 P65

■シールリボンでラッピング

■リボンで作ったスイーツ

■クリスマスプレゼント

■ルームアクセサリー

■多色リボンでラッピング　　■ペーパーバックも手作りで　　■ウェディングプレゼントアルバム

■サマーギフトに　　■インテリア小物にリボンで飾る

■ バタフライローズ
■ 星の枝

Butterfly Rose/Star Branch

ベトナムの売り子さんに大きな花束を。
こんなにうれしそうな表情に。
材料 P51・P56　型紙 P69・P70

■ 夏のバラ

Summer Rose

アンコールワット、プノン・バケンの山の上からブルーのペーパーでラッピング。
材料 P48　型紙 P64

■ カサブランカ・
　オリジナル

Casa Blanca Original

遺跡アンコールトムに、可憐な白いカサブランカが映えて。
材料 P50　型紙 P68

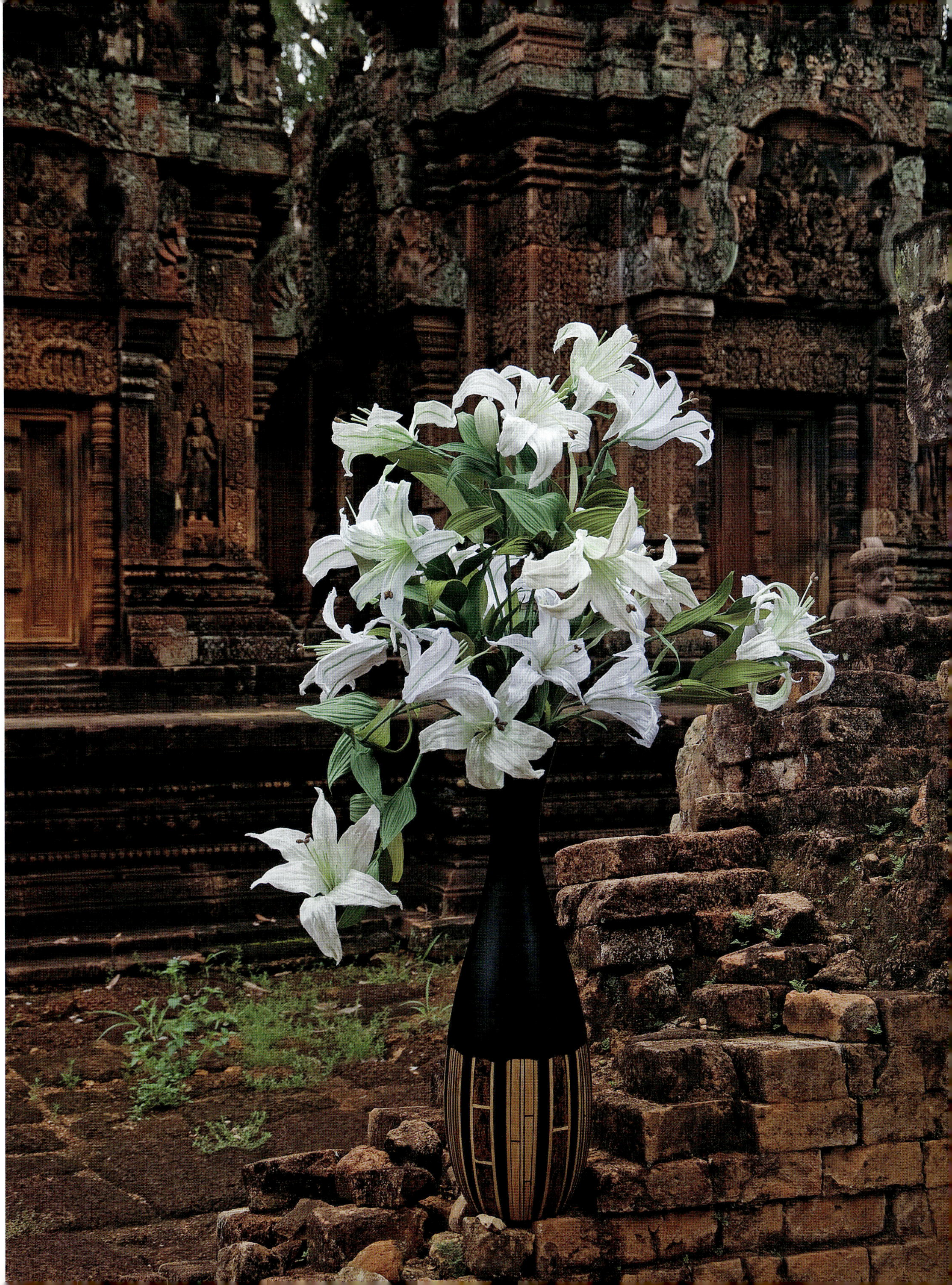

■ ミモザ
mimosa
平和を祈って、ベトナムで戦車の上へミモザの花束を。
材料 P55　型紙 P65

■オーガンジーのばら
Organdy-Rose

アンコールワットの前では、
花もかごの中の小人のように。
材料 P54　型紙 P71

■ポップコーン　■スターチス
■コインリーフ　■ベアグラス

**Popcorn/Statice/
Coin Leaf/Beargrass**

アンティークカラーで多くの花々をまとめ、
アンコールトムの庭先に置いてシックな感じを
材料 P56・P60　型紙 P70・P73・P74

材料　MATERIAL

■小さい菊の花　Small Daisy　☐写真（PHOTO）P41　☐型紙（PATTERN）P65

	花弁(PETAL)	葉(LEAF)	がく(SEPAL)	花芯(CORE)	茎(STEM)	その他(MISC)
リボン RIBBON	アートサテン14 or 02／コットンバルーア01／シルキー01 アートサテン02／コットンバルーア04／シルキー02 Art Satin14 or 02／Velour01／Silky01 Art Satin02／Velour04／Silky02	アートサテン28 or 41／シルキー05 Art Satin28 or 41／Silky05	アートサテン28 or 41／シルキー05 Art Satin28 or 41／Silky05	10mm素ボール ウールコード05 バラペップ（黄） 10mm styrofoam ball wool code 05 rose stamen（yellow）	アートサテン28 or 41 Art Satin28 or 41	葉は2枚づつ付ける Add two leaves at once
ワイヤー WIRE	#28白地巻き1/4 20枚 #28　White covered 1/4	#26白地巻き1/2 16枚 #26　White covered 1/2		#22白地巻きワイヤー 10mmの素ボールにボンドを付けてさす 素ボールの周りにウールコードを付けさらに15本を半分にカットしたバラペップを高めにつける #22　White covered Place #22 wire into the ball Place the wool code around the ball and them Put rose-stamens		
こて IRON	弁ごて シルキー側から No-lined iron from Silky side	三筋ごて シルキー側から Three lined iron from Silky side	三筋ごて シルキー側から Three lined iron from Silky side			

■風のアジサイ　Wind Hydrangea　☐写真（PHOTO）P41　☐型紙（PATTERN）P65

	花弁(PETAL)	花芯(CORE)	その他(MISC)
リボン RIBBON	ラビアン23／シルキーオンブレ13,26,32,39／オーガンジーオンブレ23 ラビアン23 or オーガンジーオンブレ23／シルキーオンブレ13,26,32,39／シルキー03,07,23,37,38,39,44,47,57,61,68 Lavien 23／Silky OMbre13,26,32,39／Organdy Ombre23 Lavien 23 or Organdy Ombre23／Silky Ombre13,26,32,39／Silky03,07,23,37,38,39,44347,57,61,68 ラビアン23 or オーガンジーオンブレ23／シルキーオンブレ13,26,32,39／アートサテン（裏出し）07,37 Lavien 23 or Organdy Ombre23／Silky Ombre13,26,32,39／Art Stin（Wrong side）07,37	あじさいペップ シルキー45でペップの茎をあらかじめ巻く 3mm幅 Hydrangea Stamen Wrap the stem with Silky 45	・同色系花弁 8 枚くらいをひとまとめにし、#22ワイヤーを添えシルキー45で半分ほど巻きおろす ・色目に気をつけながら、束ねて更にシルキー 45 で巻きおろす ・葉を作る時は 7.2×7.2 正方の大きさでアートサテン 28 or 41 裏だしにシルキー 45、三筋ごて Bundle Simmilar color of petals (8pieces) with #22wire,and wrap the stem with Silky 45 Consider the coloring, bundle all petals together and wrap the stem with Silky45
こて IRON	弁ごて どちら側からあてても良い ひっくり返して中心 No-lined iron from any side Flip over and center		

■夏のバラ　Summer Rose　☐写真（PHOTO）P44　☐型紙（PATTERN）P64

	花弁(PETAL)	葉(LEAF)	がく(SEPAL)	花芯(CORE)	その他(MISC)
リボン RIBBON	シルキー08／シルキー05／ワイヤー／ラビアン10 シルキー08／シルキー32／ワイヤー／ラビアン10 Silky08／Silky 05／Wire／Lavien10 Silky08／Silky 32／Wire／Lavien10	シール32／ アートサテン07 3枚葉 5枚葉 Seal 32／ Art Satin 07 3 leaf set 5 leaf set	シルキー08／08 Silky 08／08	ツートンペップ 20本を2つ折 Two-tone Stamen 20 Pieces folded in half	コットン cotton
ワイヤー WIRE	ワイヤーのまわりのみボンド #28ワイヤーをシルキー08であらかじめ巻いたものを花弁で使用する Place glue around the wire only Wrap #28wire with Silky 08 for Lamination	#24白地巻き #24White Covered			
こて IRON	三筋ごて ラビアン側から Three-lined iron from Lavien	三筋ごて アートサテン側から Three-lined iron from Art satin	ひねり Twist by hand		
MEMO	花弁4枚で花芯まわり→次の6枚は左右のみ（バタフライのように付ける）→10枚目から左右に少しずらす→そのまわりを残りの花弁で丸く付けていく Use 4 petals to place around the core → Place next 6 petals right and left position →Place last 10 petals to make round shape.				

■火の鳥　Fire Bird　□写真（PHOTO）P16　□型紙（PATTERN）P67

	花弁（PETAL）	がく①（SEPAL①）	がく②（SEPAL②）	その他（MISC）
リボン RIBBON	ラビアン16／16 #28 1/2ワイヤーのみボンド20枚 シルキー16／16 #26 1/2ワイヤーはさみ貼合せ8枚 きらめきピンキー16／シルキー16 #26 1/2ワイヤーはさみ貼合せ6枚 バルーア16／シール86 #24 1/2ワイヤーはさみ貼合せ8枚 シール86／アートサテン16 #24 1/2ワイヤーはさみ貼合せ8枚 Lavien 16／16　Put glue only the #28 1/2 wire（20pieces） Silky 16／16　Laminate with #26 1/2 wire（8pieces） kirameki Pinky 16／Silky16　Laminate with #26 1/2 wire（6pieces） Valour16／Seal 86 Laminate with #24 1/2 wire（8pieces） Seal 86／Art Satin 16 Laminate with #24 1/2 wire（8pieces）	アートサテン16／シルキー16 6枚 子房より4cmくらい下部に 6枚一度に付ける Art Satin 16／Silky 16 6pieces Place 6sepals 4cm below from the cotto ovary	アートサテン16／シルキー16 2枚 Art Satin 16 ／Silky 16 2pieces	ステム…アートサテン16裏出し 花芯…ペップ1/3量を2/3の長さにカットし、#26ワイヤーで束ね、シルキーで巻いておく コットンで子房を大きく作る Stem…Art Satin 16 （Wrong side will be shown） Flower core …Use 1/3 stamens. Cut 1/3 long and bundle together with #26 wire wrap stem with silky Cotton…to make ovary
こて IRON	三筋ごて 表・裏両方から 上から下へ Three-lined iron both right and wrong side of ribbon	筋ごて サテン側よりがくの形にそって 外側のワイヤーのわき Knife-shaped iron from Satin side	三筋ごて シルキー側から Three-lined iron from Silky side	
MEMO	花弁は①ラビアンの花弁→②シルキーの花弁→③きらめきピンキーの花弁→④バルーア／シールの花弁とシール／アートサテンの花弁を混ぜて→⑤カシミールの花弁の順につける Place petal①Lavien Petals→②Silky petals →③Kirameki Pinky petals→④Mix Valour/Seal and Seal/Satin petals			

■水色の涙　Blue Tears　□写真（PHOTO）P37　□型紙（PATTERN）P66

	花弁（PETAL）	葉（LEAF）	実（BERRY）	茎（STEM）
リボン RIBBON	アートサテン07／ シルキー08 9枚 Art Satin07／ Silky 08 9 pieces	アートサテン07／シルキー08／葉（小） シール32／アートサテン07／葉（大） Art Satin07／Silky08／Leaf（Small） Seal32／Art Satin07／Leaf（Large）	10mm素ボール #26ワイヤー（3本）にシルキー08を3mm幅にカットし巻いておく ウールコード（白） 10mm styro foam ball Wrap the #26wire with Silky 08 make 3pieaces wool code	シール32 表出しで逆だてる seal32 wrong side will be shown
ワイヤー WIRE		#26白地巻き #24白地巻き #26 White covered #24 White covered	素ボールのボンド→ウールコードをつける→がくをつける→ 1/3にカットしたワイヤーをさす Add glue to ball with wool code → Place the Sepal→Place the stem with Silky	
こて IRON	玉ごて（3分） シルキー側から丸くなるように Round-shaped iron from silky side	筋ごて 両面上から下へあてる Knife-shaped iron both sides		
MEMO	9個の実を順に束ね途中で#24ワイヤーを入れる 葉は小5枚を1cm間隔で向かい合わせに付け、葉（大）はシールを内側にして同様 全体は75cmほど		Bundle 9 berries together with #24 wires, Place 5 small leaves, and then large leaves.	

■キャベツローズ　Cabbage Roses　□写真（PHOTO）P18　□型紙（PATTERN）P67

	花弁（PETAL）	花芯（CORE）
リボン RIBBON	コットンバルーア05／シルキー05　大5枚小4枚 シルキー05／05　小3枚 シルキー05／グリッターバブルドットライム07　大5枚 Cotton Valour 05／Silky05　Large 5pieces,Small4pieces Silky 05／05 Silky 05／Glitter Babble Dot(9179-07) Large 5 pieces	ミレーネ10 おたふくペップ シルバー Mirene Ribbon10 Otafuku Stamen (Silver)
ワイヤー WIRE	#22白地巻き #22White covered	
こて IRON	三筋ごて シルキー側から Three-lined iron from Silky side	

材料　MATERIAL

■カサブランカオリジナル　Casa Blanca Original　□写真（PHOTO）P45　□型紙（PATTERN）P68

	花弁(PETAL)	葉(LEAF)	茎(STEM)	花芯(CORE)
リボン RIBBON	シール01／シルキーオンブレー05 アートサテン01／シルキーオンブレー05 アートサテン01／シルキー01 #22白地巻きワイヤー Seal01／Silky Ombre05 Art Satin01／Silky Ombre05 Art Satin01／Silky 01	アートサテン28 or 41 or 29／ シルキー28 or 41 Art Satin28 or 41 or 29／ Silky28 or 41	シルキー41 Silky41	シルキー20 ペップ3本の頭のみをシルキー20で巻き、 ステムを5mm残してカットし、#22を添える silky20 Wrap 3 Stamens top with Silky 20 Cut the Excess wire off and place #22wire
ワイヤー WIRE	15cmほどステムテープ（白）を先が細くなる ように巻く。さらにその上からシルキー05を 巻く（6本作る）花弁リボンと貼り合わす Wrap the wire with Stem tape (White) and then wrap with Silky 05 Make 6 pieces Use the wire for lamination	#24白地巻きワイヤー 葉はサテンとシルキー好きな 組み合わせで1本の中に色が まざるように #24White covered Any color willbe use for leaf		ポプリンオンブレー05 1、2cm幅のバイアスにカットし、斜襟こてに通す （7本9cmにカット） Poplin ombre05 Cut the ribbon1,2cm wire, and use Shakei-iron Make 7 pieces
こて IRON	ひねり Twist by hand	筋ごて Knife-shaped iron		#24にボンドをつけ、中に通す 1本はペップがついているものを通す place#24wire into the stem

■マルチカラーローズ　Multi color rose　□写真（PHOTO）P14　□型紙（PATTERN）P69

	花弁(PETAL)	葉(LEAF)	がく(SEPAL)	ステム(STEM)	その他(MISC)
リボン RIBBON	オンブレー13,32,26,15,39,05 シルキー 37,07,15,23,39,44 Silky Ombre13,32,26,15,39,05 Silky 37,07,15,23,39,44 この組み合わせの中から4〜6色で花を作る	アートサテン41／37 両方とも裏出し Art Satin 41／37 wrong side of ribbon will be shown	アートサテン41／37 両方とも裏出し Art Satin41／37 wrong side will be shown	アートサテン37 裏出し Art Satin 37 wrong side of ribbon will be shown	バラ芯（大） コットン Rose core (large) cotton
ワイヤー WIRE	#26白地巻きワイヤー ワイヤーなし10枚 ワイヤーあり10枚 #26White covered with wire 10pieces without wire 10 pieces	#24白地巻きワイヤー #24White covered 8 pieces			
こて IRON	ひねり Twisted by hand	三筋ごて グリーン側から表に返してワイヤーの 上にもあてる Three-lined iron from green color of ribbon	ひねり 紫が外側になるように Twisted by hand Purple color will be shown outside		

■まじょのどくいちご　Majo-Majo Strawberry　□写真（PHOTO）P5・P17・P40　□型紙（PATTERN）P69

	実(BERRY)	がく(SEPAL)	茎(STEM)	その他(MISC)
リボン RIBBON	アートサテン15 シルキー56 オーガンジー58 ラビアン16 Art Satin15 Silky 56 Lavien 16 Organdy58	アートサテン41／ シルキー41 表出し Art Satin41／ Silky 41 shown wrong side	#28白地巻き #28White covered	72mm正方リボンで素ボールを巻きこてをあてる wrap the ball with 7.2×7.2 Squar ribbon
ワイヤー WIRE	25mm素ボール 25mm Styrofoam ball			
こて IRON	わすれなごて Flower shaped iron	1筋ごて シルキー側から One-lined iron from silky side		
MEMO	Wrap the strofoam ball with the berry ribbon and press the berry with the Flower-shaped iron			

■なごみ　Nagomi　□写真（PHOTO）P40　□型紙（PATTERN）P67

	花弁（PETAL）	葉（LEAF）	茎（STEM）	花芯（CORE）	その他（MISC）
リボン RIBBON	ラビアン23／アートサテン14／シルキー14 Lavien 23／Art Satin14／Silky14	シルキー44／44 Silky44／44	シルキー44 Silky 44	素玉ペップワイヤーステムをシルキー44で巻いておく White stamen with wire Wrap the stem with stem with Silky44	花の立ち上がりを4～5cmにし、30輪をシルキー44で組んでいく途中、葉（小）（中）（大）を入れていくこれを3～5作る Bundle 30 flowers with silky. Add S. M, L Size leaves. Make 3～5 branches to finish
ワイヤー WIRE		#28白地巻きワイヤー #28White covered wire			
こて IRON	わすれな草こて（ラビアン側から） Flower-shaped iron from Lavien side	筋ごて （ななめ外からワイヤーへ） Knife-shaped iron (outer edge to the wire)			

■バタフライローズ　Butterfly Rose　□写真（PHOTO）P44　□型紙（PATTERN）P69

	花弁（PETAL）	葉（LEAF）	茎（STEM）	がく（SEPAL）	その他（MISC）
リボン RIBBON	ラビアン03,23／オーガンジー38,05／ラビアン03,23いずれかの組み合わせで3枚貼 Lavien 03,23／Orgabdy38,05／Lavien03,23 Any colorof ribbon to chose for lamination	アートサテン41（裏出し）／シルキー29（50mm×50mm正方）葉ステム　シルキー　アートサテン（裏出し）どちらでも Art Satin 41／Silky29 Satin will be shown wrong side	アートサテン41（裏出し） Art Satin 41 Satin will be shown wrong side	アートサテン41（裏出し）／シルキー29 Art Satin 41／Silky29 Satin will be shown wrong side	ペップ1/4束を#26で留め、シルキー29で巻いておくワイヤーなし花弁は表、裏混ぜてボンドをつける ワイヤーあり花弁はワイヤーが見えない側にボンドをつける use 1/4 pieces of stamens and wrap with silky29 place petalA,B and C, any side around the stamens
ワイヤー WIRE	#28白地巻き1/2小6枚、中10枚、大10枚（ワイヤーなし）小10枚、大10枚（ワイヤー有） #28white covered	三筋ごて 3枚葉／5枚葉 #28white covered			
こて IRON	3分玉ごて 表、裏押す様に上部から真ん中くらいまで Round -shaped A-6　　D-10 B-10　　E-10 C-10	三筋ごて Three-lined		ひねり Twisted by hand	
MEMO	最初の花弁はペップあ隠れる様に花弁を広げず（立てるようにつける）#30裸ワイヤーで位置を決めながらできあがりは丸くならないように気をつける。両サイドに花弁が多めに来るように Place all petal to make a shape as butterfly				

■サンバドロップ　Samba-Drop　□写真（PHOTO）P28　□型紙（PATTERN）P70

	実（BERRY）	葉（LEAF）	茎（STEM）	がく（SEPAL）	つぼみ（BUD）	その他（MISC）
リボン RIBBON	シール01,23,04,32,39,16,31,17混ぜて作る 8色で1枝 3.6×3.6正方形 Seal 01,23,04,32,39,16,31,17 Mix all 8colors to make 1branch	サテン（裏出し）41／シルキー41 8枚 Satin41／ Silky41 Art Satin will be shown wrong side	シルキー41　2mm幅 #28ワイヤーにステムを巻き1/3にカットして実にボンドをつけ、さす 全体ステム　シルキー41 Silky41 Wrap #28 wire with Silky 41 Cut into 3 and peek to the berry	サテン41（裏出し）／シルキー41 実1個に2枚必要 Art Satin 41／Silky41 Art Satin will be shown wrong side	ペップ5本2つ折りボンドをつけ#28で括るがく2枚つけるステム→シルキー41 Two-tone stamen Bundle 5 stamens in half and place 2 Sepal	実はとがった方が下側になるがくは1枚目は実に沿うように貼る 2枚目は下付になるように
ワイヤー WIRE	ワイヤー#28白地巻き #28white covered wire	#26白地巻き1/2 #26white covered wire				
こて IRON	十字になるようにつき合わせて貼り余分をカット Dongri Styrofoam ball	三筋ごて シルキー側から上→下 表に返して中心 Three-lined iron from Silky		三筋ごて シルキー側から中心へシルキー側だけ Three-lined iron from silky		
MEMO	つぼみをトップに。10cm下に7～8cmの立ち上がりの実を付ける。その後2cm間隔で実を入れ、3個目に葉。実、葉を繰り返し、残りの葉を入れ、ステムを強化しながら全体を75cm～80cmで仕上げる。実の色順は自由。 Place bud at first, add 3berris and leaf. Repeat the same process to finish.					

材料 MATERIAL

■春一番　First Spring Breeze　□写真（PHOTO）P31　□型紙（PATTERN）P69

	花弁（PETAL）	葉（LEAF）	がく（SEPAL）	花芯（CORE）	その他（MISC）
リボン RIBBON	シルキー44,02,05,07,23,37 シングルでカットする 2～3枚で1輪15 Silky 44,02,05,07,23,37 No lamination 2～3 pieces make 1 flower need to be 15flowers	シルキー44／44 10枚 Silky 44／44 10 pieces	コットンバルーア01／ シルキー01 貼り合わせ 1枚で1輪15、1枚 Cotton Velour 01／ Silky 01 1piece for 1 flower need to be 15 piece	素玉にペップ 黄色に染める ステムをシルキー44で巻く White top stamen Wrap the stem with silky 44	シルキー花弁（2枚or 3枚）をペップに通した後にがく（貼り合わせ1枚）を通す。これを15輪ほど作る。 Stroke 2～3petals to the stamen and place sepal To make 15 flowers
ワイヤー WIRE		#26白地巻きワイヤー1/2 #26white covered wire			
こて IRON	すずらんごて シルキー側からひっくり返さない Suzuran iron iron from Silky side	三筋ごて 上から下へ Three-lined iron	すずらんごて シルキー側からひっくり返さない Suzuran iron iron from Silky side		
MEMO	最初の花下1cmの所に#24ワイヤー3本足し、ステム（シルキー44）で巻きおろす。1cm間隔で花をつけた。（途中#24ワイヤーを状況に合わせて足す）葉は1cm間隔で10枚つける。 Place three #24wire 1cm under of the first flower and wrap with Silky 44 Place rest of the flower 1cm each space				

■マルチカラーフラワー　Multi Color Flower　□写真（PHOTO）P7　□型紙（PATTERN）P70

	花弁（PETAL）	葉（LEAF）	茎（STEM）	花芯（CORE）	がく（SEPAL）	その他（MISC）
リボン RIBBON	シルキー8,10,98,32,22,39,5 色々な色の貼り合わせ 50～60枚 Silky8,10,98,32,22,39,5 Laminate with any colors 50～60 pieces	シール33／シルキー33 3枚葉 5枚葉 Seal33／Silky 33 3-Leaf set 5-Leaf set	シルキー33 Silky 33	ゆりペップ 黄色に染める 片落し シルキー33で巻く 6本 Lily stamen Wrap the stem with silky 33 6 pieces	シルキー33／33 Silky 33／33	コットン cotton
ワイヤー WIRE	#26白地巻1/3 #26white covered 1/3	#24白地巻1/2 #24 White covered1/2				
こて IRON	三筋ごて 好きな色のシルキー側 Three-lined iron any color of Silky side	三筋ごて シール、シルキー側の順 Three-lined iron seal first and Silky side			ひねり Twisted by hands	
MEMO	花芯6本をひとまとめにし、回りに花弁をつける Bundle 6 stamens together and place 5～60pieces of petal around the core					

■ブラックカトリーヌ　Black Catherine　□写真（PHOTO）P4　□型紙（PATTERN）P70

	花弁（PETAL）	葉（LEAF）	花芯（CORE）	MEMO
リボン RIBBON	シール33／シルキー33 シール01／サテン02 バルーア33／サテン16 シルキー33／サテン25 バルーア01／サテン14 貼り合わせ Seal 33／Silky 33 Seal 01／Art Satin 02 Velour 33／Art Satin 16 Seal 33／Art Satin25 Velour 01／Art Satin 14	シルキー33 シルキー01 シルキー33 シルキー01 Silky 33 Silky 01 Silky 33 Silky 01	イバラペップ（黄色） 5本、2折 Rose stamen（yellow） 5 pieces bend in half	花芯の周りに花弁A、その間に花弁B 10輪 花芯の周りに花弁C、その周りに花弁D 5輪 15輪を使ってこんもり盛り上がるようにまとめる Place petal A around the core and then place petal B in between →10 flowers Place petal C around the core and then place petal D in between →5 flowers The 15 flowers bundle together to make a big flower
ワイヤー WIRE	#26白地巻1/3 #26 White covered1/3 花弁A,B 各3枚1輪 花弁C,D 3枚／5枚 Petal A・B 3pieces Petal C・D 3pieces/5 pieaces	#24白地巻き #24White Covered		
こて IRON	弁ごて（大）シルキー側から No-lined iron from Silky side			

■ダイヤローズ　Diamond Rose　□写真（PHOTO）P27・P32　□型紙（PATTERN）P71

	花弁①(PETAL)	花弁②(PETAL)	花弁③(PETAL)	葉(LEAF)	がく(SEPAL)	その他(MISC)
リボン RIBBON	シール39／シルキー47 シール16／シルキー46 シール31／シルキー63 シール01／シルキー44 シール33／シルキー33,46,47 Seal39／Silky47 Seal16／Silky46 Seal31／Silky63 Seal01／Silky44 Seal33／Silky33,46,47	50mm×9mm　16枚 60mm×18mm　16枚 65mm×18mm　16枚 72mm×18mm　20枚 ワイヤーあり	24mm×36mm　3枚 36mm×36mm　6枚 45mm×36mm　4枚 ワイヤーなし	アートサテン29（裏出し）／ シルキー29 3枚葉・5枚葉 Art Satin 29／ Silky 29 Satin will be shown wrong side	シルキー29／29 Silky29／29	バラ芯（小）#24を3本通す 24mm×36mm花弁は花芯を つつむようにつける コットン Rose core (small) Cotton
ワイヤー WIRE	#28白地巻き #28 White covered			#26白地巻きワイヤー1/2 #26 White covered1/2		
こて IRON	弁ごて ワイヤーあり：シルキー側 シール側混ぜて No-lined iron from Silky or Seal side to make mix0	弁ごて（ワイヤーなし） 24mm→シルキー側から 36mm→シルキー側から 45mm→混ぜる No-lined iron 24mm→Silky side 36mm→Silky side 45mm→Mix		三筋ごて Three-lined iron	ひねり Twisted by hand	
MEMO	ベタ貼りの花弁はシルキー側からボンド 小3枚で一回り。立ち上がり1cm。中、大も同様。ワイヤー入り花弁はシール側からボンド。小→中→大の順。最後の72mm花弁は花の下を覆うようにつける。 Start with 24mm×36mmPetal Use 3 small petals to around the core. Petal (M), Petal (L), repeat same procedure as small. Put glue on Seal side for Petal with wire.					

■ブルーライトフラワー　Blue Light Flower　□写真（PHOTO）P6　□型紙（PATTERN）P72

	花弁①(PETAL)	花弁②(PETAL)	花弁③(PETAL)	葉(LEAF)	がく(SEPAL)	その他(MISC)
リボン RIBBON	花弁A（10枚） オーガンジーオンブレ32 ラビアン10／39　3枚貼り 花弁B（10枚） シルキー6,7,8,37,44 どれかで3枚貼り PetalA(10) Organdy Ombre32 Lavien10／39 PetalB（10) Silky 6,7,8,37,44	花弁C（10枚） サテン7 シルキー32／44　3枚貼り 花弁D（10枚） シルキー22／10　3枚貼り シール32 PetalC(10) Satin7 Silky32／44 PetalD （10) Silky22／10 Seal32	花弁E（10枚） バルーア22／サテン7 Petal E （10) Cotton Velour22／Satin7 各花弁10枚は色 混ぜてOK ワイヤーの位置も	サテン07（裏出し）／ シルキー22 Satin7／ Silky22 Art Satin will be shown wrong side 3枚葉 5枚葉	サテン07／ シルキー22 Satin7／ Silky22	花芯（オタフクビーズペップ・シルバー） 15本2つ折り Bends stamen silver 15 Bend in half
ワイヤー WIRE	花弁A　#28白地巻き1/2 Any 3-Silky to laminate #28White covered1/2	花弁B,C,D,E #26白地巻き1/2 Petal　B,C,D,E #26 White covered1/2		#24白地巻き1/2 サテン07（裏出し） #24White covered1/2 Satin7 Art Satin will be shown wrong side		
こて IRON	三筋ごて あちこちにあてる Three-lined iron	三筋ごて Three-lined iron	三筋ごて Three-lined iron	三筋ごて Three-lined iron	ひねり Twisted by hand	
MEMO	花芯の周りに花弁Aから順につける。色、花弁の向きは自由。全体ステムはサテン07、裏だし Place petal Ato E around The core Stem ribbon is Art Satin 07, Wrong side will shown					

■赤ちゃんの小枝　Baby Hand Branch　□写真（PHOTO）P36　□型紙（PATTERN）P70

	葉(LEAF)	茎(STEM)	その他(MISC)	
リボン RIBBON	シルキー05/29　または オーガンジー05 シルキー05 Silky 05/29 or Organdy 05 Silky 05	シルキー05 Silky 05	1　葉の形にリボンをカットし、葉の中心のみにボンドをつけ、貼り合わせる。 2　葉の中心部分にワイヤーを挟む。 3　三筋ごてをあてる。またはボンドがかわかないうちにひねる。 4　バランスを見ながら、葉をつける。 5　④を何本か作り、ガーランドにする。 6　目打ちでステムをカールする。 枝にする際ワイヤー#24/22を足していく。ステムはシルキー05。 1.　Cut ribbon according to the pattern 2.　Apply glue only the center of leaves 3.　Place the wire in between 4.　Using iron to make leaves look natural or before glue has set twist them To make long branch, add #24 and #22 wires to make stem strong. Using Silky 05 for stem ribbon	
ワイヤー WIRE		#24／22 白地巻き#24／22 White-covered		
こて IRON	三筋ごてまたは　ひねり Three-line ironorTwist by hands			

・53

材料 MATERIAL

■オーガンジーのバラ　Organdy-Rose　□写真（PHOTO）P36・P47　□型紙（PATTERN）P71

	花弁(PETAL)	葉(LEAF)	がく(SEPAL)	花芯(CORE)	茎(STEM)	その他(MISC)
リボン RIBBON	オーガンジーオンブレー15 or 23 オーガンジー14 or 15 or 04 貼り合わせなしのシングルで Organdy Ombre15 or 23 Organdy14 or 15 or 04 No Lamination	マイルドカラー29／20 MildColor29／20	マイルドカラー29／20 MildColor29／20	バラ芯（小） コットン Rose core small cotton	シルキー29 Silky29	
ワイヤー WIRE		#26白地巻きワイヤー #26White covered wire				
こて IRON	玉ごて・手で先をカール Round-Shaped iron and curl by hand.	三筋ごて 3枚葉、5枚葉 Three-line iron Three-leaf set, Five leaf set	ひねり Twist			

■フリージア　FREESIA
□写真（PHOTO）P36　□型紙（PATTERN）P73

	花弁(PETAL)	葉(LEAF)	がく(SEPAL)	花芯(CORE)	茎(STEM)
リボン RIBBON	シルキー　02/02 シルキー　01/01 シルキー　04/04 Silky 02/02 Silky 01/01 Silky 04/04	シルキー　28/28 Silky 28/28	ロマンカラー66 Roman color66	バラ芯ペップ黄 Rose-stamen yellow	シルキー　29 Silky 29
こて IRON	弁ごて No-lined iron	三筋ごて Three-lined iron	弁ごて No-lined iron		

■ライラック　Lilac
□写真（PHOTO）P11・P36　□型紙（PATTERN）P72

	花弁(PETAL)	葉(LEAF)	花芯(CORE)	茎(STEM)
リボン RIBBON	ポプリン01／ ジョゼッテ44 アートサテン01／ シルキー01 Poplin01／ Josette44 Art Satin01／ Silky01	シルキー29 シルキーオンブレー44 Silky29／ Silky Ombre44	ツートンペップ Two-tone stamen	シルキー　29 Silky 29
こて IRON	三筋ごて、ポプリン or アートサテン側 Three-lined iron, from Poplin or Josette side	ひねり Twist by hand		

■マーガレット　Farguerite　□写真（PHOTO）P36　□型紙（PATTERN）P71

	花弁(PETAL)	葉(LEAF)	がく(SEPAL)	花芯(CORE)	茎(STEM)	その他(MISC)
リボン RIBBON	ラビアン61 or 03／ アートサテン01 or 02／ シルキー01 or 02 Lavien61 or 03／ Art Stain01 or 02／ Silky01 or 02	ラビアン10／ アートサテン29／ シルキー29 Lavien10／ Art Satin29／ Silky29	ラビアン10／ アートサテン29／ シルキー29 Lavien10 Art Satin29 Silky29	シルキー04/04 シルキー29/29 ボンテン（黄） 糸芯ペップ（白） ボンテン→シルキー（04） →糸芯ペップ→シルキー（29） Silky29 Silky04/04 Silky29/29 Boten, Yellow White Stamen Bonten_Silky04_Stamen_Silky29	シルキー29 Silky29	
ワイヤー WIRE	#28白地巻きワイヤー1/3 #28 White covered wire 1/3	#26白地巻きワイヤー1/2 #26 White covered wire				
こて IRON	三筋ごて（ラビアン側から） Three-lined iron, from Lavien side	三筋ごて（シルキー側から） Three-lined iron, from Silky side	三筋ごて（シルキー側から） Three-lined iron, from Silky side			

■チューリップ Tulip □写真（PHOTO）P10・P36 □型紙（PATTERN）P73

	花弁(PETAL)	葉(LEAF)	花芯(CORE)	茎(STEM)	その他(MISC)
リボン RIBBON	アートサテン16（裏出し）／ オーガンジーオンブレー13 Art Satin16／ Organdy Ombre13 Wrong side of Art Satin will be shown	アートサテン41／ シルキー29 Art Satin41／ Silky29	シルキー29 ツートンペップ #26白地巻きワイヤー ペップ3本を二つ折りにし、ワイヤーを足してシルキーで10cm巻く Silky29 Two-tone Stamen #26 White coverd wire Fold 3 stamens in half, add wire the stem （10cm）	アートサテン41裏出し たて巻き Art Satin41 Wrong side or Art Satin will be shown Vertically wrap	チューリップ、カラーバリエーション アートサテン02（裏出し）／オーガンジー アートサテン63（裏出し）／オーガンジーオンブレー アートサテン15（裏出し）／オーガンジー13 アートサテン01／オーガンジー アートサテン14（裏出し）／オーガンジーオンブレー14 Tulip color Art Satin02／Organdy04 Art Satin63／Organdy Ombre43 Art Satin01／Organdy01 Art Satin15／Organdy Ombre13 Art Satin14／Organdy Ombre14 Art Satin Will be shown wrong side
ワイヤー WIRE	#26白地巻きワイヤー #26 White coverd wire	#24白地巻きワイヤー #24 White covered wire			
こて IRON	弁ごて（オーガンジー側から） 玉ごて（オーガンジー側・中心） No-lined iron, from Organdy side Round-shaped iron, from Organdy side	ひねり Twist by hand			

■キャロ君のバラ Caro-Rose
□写真（PHOTO）P9・P19 □型紙（PATTERN）P72

	花弁(PETAL)	葉(LEAF)	がく(SEPAL)	茎(STEM)	その他(MISC)
リボン RIBBON	ラビアン16／ シルキー16／ シルキー55 Lavien16／ Silky16／ Silky55	ラビアン46／ シルキー29／ シルキー41 Lavien46／ Silky29／ Silky41	ラビアン46／ シルキー29／ シルキー41 Lavien46／ Silky29／ Silky41	シルキー Silky41	バラ芯（小） コットン Rose-core small cotton
ワイヤー WIRE		#26白地巻きワイヤー #26 White be covered wire			
こて IRON	ひねり Twist by hand	三筋ごて、シルキー側から 3枚葉、5枚葉 Three-lined iron, from Silky side Three-leaf set, Five-leaf set	ひねり Twist by hand		

■ミモザ mimosa
□写真（PHOTO）P46 □型紙（PATTERN）P65

	実(BERRY)	葉(LEAF)	茎(STEM)
リボン RIBBON	ボンテン（黄） 12〜15個 Bonten（Yellow） 12〜15pieces	ロマンカラー66／ シルキー29 7枚葉を組む Roman Color66／ Silky29 7 Leaf set	シルキー29 Silky29
ワイヤー WIRE	#26グリーンワイヤー #26 Green-covered wire	#26 白地巻ワイヤー #26 White-covered wire	
こて IRON		三筋ごて 貼り合わせは、 ワイヤーのみボンド Three-lined iron Put glue only the wire and laminate together.	

■ガーベラ Gerbera □写真（PHOTO）P9・P22 □型紙（PATTERN）P74

	花弁(PETAL)	がく(SEPAL)	花芯(CORE)	茎(STEM)	その他(MISC)
リボン RIBBON	コットンバルーア01／ シルキー01 Cotton Velour01 Silky01	コットンバルーア01／ シルキー01 Cotton Velour01 Silky01	コットンバルーア04／ シルキー04 コットンバルーア33／ シルキー33 Cotton Velour04 Silky04 Cotton Velour33 Silky33	コットンバルーア01（裏出し） Cotton Velour01 Wrong side will be shown	花芯（大）黒　花芯（小）黄 Flower-core（L） Black Flower-core（S） Yellow
ワイヤー WIRE	#30白地巻きワイヤー #30 White covered wire			縦巻き Wrap the stem vertically	
こて IRON	三筋ごて、シルキー側から Three-lined iron, from Silky side	三筋ごて、シルキー側から Three-lined iron, from Silky side			

材料 MATERIAL

■コインリーフ　Coin Leafr
□写真（PHOTO）P46　　□型紙（PATTERN）P74

	コインリーフ(COIN LEAFR)
リボン RIBBON	シルキー61/61 シルキー32/32 #28のワイヤーをシルキーで巻く。 そのワイヤーで丸い形を作り、リボンで挟んで貼る。 Silky61/61 Silky32/32 Wrap #28 wire with Silky. Make the circle with the wire and laminate it with same color ribbons

■スターチス　Statice
□写真（PHOTO）P46　　□型紙（PATTERN）P74

	花弁(PETAL)	がく(SEPAL)	茎(STEM)
リボン RIBBON	シルキー39、57、04 シングルのままで Silky39、57、04 No lamination	シルキー20 シングルのままで Silky20 No lamination	シルキー20 縦巻き Silky20 Wrap the stem vertically
ワイヤー WIRE	#28　白地巻きワイヤー #28 White covered wire	花弁とがくを合わせ、中心に#28ワイヤーをかけギャザーをよせる。 Bundle petal and sepal together and wrap with #28 wire to make gather	
こて IRON	ひねり Twist by hands		

■星の枝　Star Branch
□写真（PHOTO）P44　　□型紙（PATTERN）P70

	花弁(PETAL)	茎(STEM)
リボン RIBBON	コットンバルーア61／シルキー61 Cotton Velour61／Silky61	シルキー61 Silky61
ワイヤー WIRE		ワイヤー入りゆりペップ Lily stamen with wire
こて IRON	一筋ごて、シルキー側から、表に反して中心 One-lined iron, from Silky side, flip over then center	

■ポップコーン　Popcorn
□写真（PHOTO）P46　　□型紙（PATTERN）P70

	花弁(PETAL)	茎(STEM)	花芯(CORE)
リボン RIBBON	コットンバルーア61／シルキー21 コットンバルーア30／シルキー21 コットンバルーア35／シルキー21 Cotton Velour61／Silky21 Cotton Velour30／Silky21 Cotton Velour35／Silky21	コットンバルーア35（裏出し） Cotton Velour35 Wrong side of ribbon, will be shown	ツートンペップ Two-tone stamen
こて IRON	すずらんごて、シルキー側から Suzuran iron, from Silky		

■パリのラナンキュラス　Ranunculus in Paris　□写真（PHOTO）P10　　□型紙（PATTERN）P77

	花弁(PETAL)	葉(LEAF)	花芯(CORE)	がく(SEPAL)	茎(STEM)
リボン RIBBON	オーガンジー14／シルキー23 花弁（A～D）は中心のみボンドで貼り合わせ、花弁（E、F）はワイヤーのみにボンド。 Organdy14／Silky 23 Petal A～D, put glue on middle, Petal E,F, put the glue only the wire	アートサテン29（裏出し） Art Satin 29 Art Satin should be shown the wrong side	シルキー29 Silky 29 24m/m1正方で丸くしたコットンを包む Wrap the cotton ball with 24_24m/m square バラペップ（グリーン） Rose stamen Green	アートサテン29／シルキー29 アートサテンは裏出し Art Satin 29／Silky 29 Art Satin should be shown the wrong side	アートサテン（裏出し） Art Satin 29 Art Satin should be shown the wrong side
ワイヤー WIRE					#24白ロングワイヤー #24 White covered Long wire
こて IRON	三筋ごて、オーガンジー側、中心 Three-lined iron, from Organdy	三筋ごて、表裏混ぜて Three-lined iron, from any side		三筋ごて、シルキー側から、裏返して中心 Three-lined iron, from Silky side, flivover and press center.	

■ミニカメリアローズ　Mini-Camellia Rose　□写真（PHOTO）P5　□型紙（PATTERN）P76

	花弁(PETAL)	葉(LEAF)	茎(STEM)	がく(SEPAL)	花芯(CORE)	その他(MISC)
リボン RIBBON	ラビアン10／ コットンバルーア05／ ラビアン10 Lavien 10／ Cotton Velour 05／ Lavien 10	アートサテン29／ シルキー29 3枚葉、5枚葉 Art Satin 29／ Silky 29 Three-leaf set, Five-leaf set	シルキー29 Silky 29	アートサテン29／ シルキー29 Art Satin 29／ Silky 29	素ボール15mm コットン用意　子房 Styrofoam ball 15mm Cotton for Ovary	①素ボールに＃24ワイヤーをつける ②全体にボンドをつけた花弁で_を包む ③中心にボンドをつけた花弁をつける ①Put ＃24 wire into the ball. ②Apply glue on petal and cover the ball. ③Apply glue on center of petal 　and place the core follow by all petals.
ワイヤー WIRE		＃24白地巻き1/2 ＃24 White-covered 1/2	＃24白地巻き ＃24 White-covered			
こて IRON	玉ごて（小） 花弁1つずつにあてる 中心も丸くなるように Round-shaped iron(S) Make round shape	三筋ごて 外側から斜め中心 返してワイヤーの上 Three-lined iron Outer edges to center and flip along wire		ひねり Twist by hands		

■ミステリーローズ　Mystery-Rose　□写真（PHOTO）P29　□型紙（PATTERN）P79

	花弁(PETAL)	葉(LEAF)	茎(STEM)	花芯(CORE)	がく(SEPAL)	その他(MISC)
リボン RIBBON	①ラビアン16／ シルキーオンブレー54／ ラビアン16 ②アートサテン16／ シルキー16 1.Lavien 16／ Silky Ombre 54／ Lavien 16 2.Art Satin 16／ Silky 16	ラビアン16／ シール16／ シルキー16 3枚葉、5枚葉 Lavien 16／ Seal 16／ Silky 16 Three-leaf set, Five-leaf set	花弁、葉で余った シルキーまたは サテンで対応 Same ribbon from leaf or petal	おたふくペップを花弁同様、 シルキーで巻いて使用する ペップのステムをシルキーで あらかじめ巻いておく Otafuku-stamens wrap with petal ribbon Wrap the stem of stamen with Silky	アートサテン10 シルキー16 アートサテン 表出し コットン用意 Art Satin 37 Silky 37 Art Satin Back side Cotton for Ovary	作り方：花弁①の根元にボンドし、20枚を3回に 分けてつける。7枚ごとに＃30ワイヤー。 花弁を2回に分けて。花弁①②とも、20枚ずつ。 色組み合わせ例： ラビアン23／シルキーオンブレー23／ラビアン23 アートサテン14／シルキー14（ピンク） ラビアン18／シルキーオンブレー17／ラビアン18 アートサテン18／シルキー18（赤紫） 1.Place 7 petals around the core. Using 　＃30uncovered wire to tide. 2.Follow by petal 2. Other color lamination: Lavien 23/Silky Ombre 23/Lavien 23: Art Satin 14/Silky 14/Lavien 18: Silky Ombre 17/Lavien 18: Art Satin 18/Silky 18
ワイヤー WIRE	＃26白地巻き1/2 ＃26 White-covered1/2	＃24白地巻き ＃24White-covered				
こて IRON	筋ごて プリーツになるように裏表 玉ごて（大） 表、中央の下 Knife-shaped iron Round-shaped iron(L)	筋ごて 外からワイヤーに向けて 表裏交互に。 花弁同様プリーツにする Knife-shaped iron Outer edges to center			ひねり Twist by hand	

■赤いカーネーション　Red-Carnation　□写真（PHOTO）P40　□型紙（PATTERN）P75

	花弁(PETAL)	葉(LEAF)	がく(SEPAL)	茎(STEM)	その他(MISC)
リボン RIBBON	シルキー16 アートサテン16 シングルのままで Silky 16 Art Satin 16 No lamination	アートサテン29／ シルキー29 Art Satin 29／ Silky 29	アートサテン29／ シルキー29 Art Satin 29／ Silky 29	シルキー Silky 29	
ワイヤー WIRE		＃26白地巻きワイヤー ＃26 White covered wire		＃22白地巻きワイヤー ＃22 White covered	
こて IRON	三筋ごて Three-lined iron シルキーの花弁を15枚 アートサテンの花弁を5枚 Silky petal 15pieces/Art Satin petal 5pieces	三筋ごて、シルキー側から Three-lined iron, from Silky side	三筋ごて、アートサテン側から Three-lined iron, from Art Satin side		

材料　MATERIAL

■日月潭
□写真（PHOTO）P39　□型紙（PATTERN）P74

	花弁（PETAL）	葉（LEAF）
リボン RIBBON	ラビアン35／ ロマンカラー63,61,62,64,65／ ラビアン35 Lavien 35／ Roman color 63,61,62,64,65／ Lavien 35	ラビアン35／ ロマンカラー66／ ラビアン35 Lavien 35／ Roman color 66／ Lavien 35
ワイヤー WIRE	ステム～ロマンカラー66 Stem～Roman color 66	#26白地巻きワイヤー #26 White covered wire
こて IRON	ひねり Twist by hand	ひねり Twist by hands 3枚葉、5枚葉 Tree-leaf set, Five-leaf set
その他 （MISC）	バラ芯（小） コットン Rose-core small Cotton	

■ローズホープ　Rose of Hope
□写真（PHOTO）P35　□型紙（PATTERN）P74

	花弁①（PETAL）	花弁②（PETAL）	葉（LEAF）
リボン RIBBON	ラビアン61／シルキー01,03,23／ラビアン61 ラビアン43／シルキー43,16／ラビアン43 ラビアン39／シルキー57／ラビアン39 Lavien61／Silky01,03,23／Lavien 61 Lavien 43／Silky　43,16／Lavien 43 Lavien 39／Silky 57／Lavien 39	ラビアン61／ シルキーオンブレ43,23,13,14／ ラビアン61 Lavien 61／ Silky Ombre 43,23,13,14／ Lavien 61	ラビアン10／ アートサテン41 or 56／ シルキー41 or 56 Lavien 10／ Art Satin 41 or 56／ Silky 41 or 56
ワイヤー WIRE			#26白地巻きワイヤー #26 White covered wire
こて IRON		ひねり Twist by hand	三筋ごて、シルキー側から 3枚葉、5枚葉 Three-lined iron from Silky side Three-leaf set, Five-leaf set
その他 （MISC）		ステム～シルキー41 or 56 バラ芯（小） コットン Stem～Silky 41 or 56 Rose-core small Cotton	

■カトレア　Cattleya　□写真（PHOTO）P20　□型紙（PATTERN）P77

	花弁（PETAL）	リップ（LIP）	がく（SEPAL）	コラム（COLUMN）	その他（MISC）
リボン RIBBON	シルキーオンブレ02／02 Silky Ombre 02／02	シルキーオンブレ02／02 Silky Ombre 02／02	シルキーオンブレ02／02 Silky Ombre 02／02	シール04 Seal 04	
ワイヤー WIRE			#24白地巻きワイヤー #24 White covered wire		
こて IRON	ひねり Twist by hands	三筋ごて、表裏から Three-lined iron from both sides	筋ごて Knife-shaped iron	三筋ごて、裏から コットン Three-lined iron from wrong side Cotton	

■プルメリア　シルキーバージョン
　Plumeria（Silky）
□写真（PHOTO）P20
□型紙（PATTERN）P64

	花弁（PETAL）
リボン RIBBON	シルキーオンブレ02／シルキー02 Silky Ombre 02／Silky 02
ワイヤー WIRE	#26白地巻きワイヤーで型紙の シェイプを作る Make the shape with #26 White Covered wire.
こて IRON	
その他 （MISC）	ワイヤー入りゆりペップ5本 Lily stemen w/wire 3.6cm

■シャネルオーキッド　Chanel Orchid
□写真（PHOTO）P20　□型紙（PATTERN）P64

	花弁（PETAL）	葉（LEAF）	茎（STEM）	花芯（CORE）
リボン RIBBON	シルキー02／04 Silky 02／04	シルキー29／28 Silky 29／28	シルキー Silky 29	ワイヤー入り素玉ペップ White top stamen w/wire
ワイヤー WIRE		#26白地巻きワイヤー #26 White Covered wire	#26白地巻きワイヤー #26 White covered wire	
こて IRON	すずらんごて 花弁（大）裏から／花弁（小）表から Suzuran iron Petal(L) from wrong side Petal(S) from right side	ひねり Twist by hands	三筋ごて、シルキー側から 3枚葉、5枚葉 Three-lined iron from Silky side Three-leaf set, Five-leaf set	

■プルメリア　Plumeria　□写真（PHOTO）P20　□型紙（PATTERN）P64

	花弁(PETAL)	茎(STEM)	作り方(FABRICATION)
リボン RIBBON	シルキーオンブレー04 コットンバルーア01 Silky Ombre04 Cotton Velour 01	シルキー29 Silky 29	1. #26ワイヤーをリボンの間に置き接着剤で貼り合わせ、型紙に合わせてカットする。 　この時リボンは下に濃い方が来るようにする。 2. へり返しごてをあてる。 3. ゆりペップ3本を2つ折りにして、黄色に染める。 4. 花芯のまわりに、花弁3枚をつける。 5. 5mm幅ステムリボンで巻きおろす。 1. Place #26 wire in between petal ribbons and laminate them together. Cut the ribbon according to the pattern. At this point, dark side of ribbon should show on the bottom of the petal. 2. Using pointed-iron stroke the shape of petal. 3. Dyeing lily-stamens with yellow color. Bend 3 lily-stamens in half and bundle together to make core. 4. Place five petals around the flower core. 5. Wrap the wire with 5mm wide stem ribbon.
ワイヤー WIRE	#26白地巻きワイヤー #26 White Covered		
こて IRON	へり返しごて Pointed-iron		
その他 (MISC)	ゆりペップ Lily-stamens		

■オーガンジーのスイートピー　Organdy Sweet pea　□写真（PHOTO）P11　□型紙（PATTERN）P76

	花弁(PETAL)	葉(LEAF)	がく(SEPAL)	茎(STEM)	花芯(CORE)	その他(MISC)
リボン RIBBON	シルキー23／ オーガンジーオンブレー23 根元のみボンドをつける Silky 23／ Organdy Ombre 23 Laminate two ribbons at the bottom only	アートサテン29／シルキー29 Art Satin 29／Silky 29	シルキー29/29 Silky 29/29	シルキー29 Silky 29	シール23 コットン Seal 23 Cotton	
こて IRON	三筋ごて、シルキー側から Three-lined iron from Silky side	三筋ごて シルキー側から Three lined iron from Silky side	三筋ごて Three-lined iron			

■シルキーのゆり　Lily　□写真（PHOTO）P12　□型紙（PATTERN）P77

	花弁(PETAL)	葉(LEAF)	茎(STEM)	花芯(CORE)
リボン RIBBON	シルキー01／43／01 Silky01／43／01	シルキー29／05 Silky29／05	シルキー29 Silky 29	ワイヤー入り ゆりペップ6本 Wired lily stamen 6 pieces
ワイヤー WIRE	#24白地巻き ワイヤー #24 White covered wire	#24白地巻き ワイヤー #24 White covered wire		茎の部分を花弁(小) のシルキーで巻く Wrap the stamen with small petal ribbon
こて IRON	ひねり Twist by hands	ひねり Twist by hands		
MEMO	花弁のシルキーは 状況に合わせて 変えてもよい。 Any Silky ribbon color will be used for petal.	葉のシルキーは 状況に合わせて、 #28、05、44等 にしてもよい。 Can use #28,05,44 Silky color.		

■シルキーサンダーソニア　Silky-Sandersonia　□写真（PHOTO）P12　□型紙（PATTERN）P79

	花弁(PETAL)	葉(LEAF)	茎(STEM)
リボン RIBBON	シルキー04／43 Silky 04／43	シルキー05／28 Silky 05／28	シルキー05 Silky 05
ワイヤー WIRE		#26白地巻きワイヤー1/2 #26 White covered wire1/2	#30白地巻きワイヤー1/2 #30ハダカワイヤー #30 White covered wire 1/2 #30 uncovered wire
こて IRON	ひねり Twist by hands		
MEMO	乾かないうちにペン等の 丸い棒に巻き付け、両端 からギャザーを寄せる。 5個作る Before the glue has set, coil the ribbon around the stick and make gathers.	大〜7枚 小〜6枚 Large 7pcs Small 6pcs	

材料　MATERIAL

■ラッパ水仙　Daffodile　□写真（PHOTO）P21　□型紙（PATTERN）P78

	花弁(PETAL)	葉(LEAF)	花芯(CORE)	苞(BRACT)	茎(STEM)	その他(MISC)
リボン RIBBON	シルキー02／02 Silky 02/02	シルキー29/28 Silky 29/28	シルキー04/03 Silky04/03	シルキー 29/28 Silky 29/28	シルキー29 Silky29	
ワイヤー WIRE	＃26白地巻きワイヤー ＃26 White-covered wire	＃26白地巻きワイヤー ＃26 White-covered wire				
こて IRON	ひねり Twist by hands	三筋ごて Three-lined iron	ワイヤー入りゆりペップ Lily stamen w/wire	ひねり Twist by hand		
MEMO			ボンドが生乾きのうちにペン等に巻き付けギャザーを寄せる。 Before the glue has set, coil the ribbon around the stick and make gathers.			

■ベアグラス　Beargrass
　□写真（PHOTO）P7・P16・P47　□型紙（PATTERN）P73

	ベアグラス(Beargrass)		その他(MISC)
リボン RIBBON	シルキー29/29（緑） シルキー33/33（黒） シルキー20/20（茶） シルキー55/55（赤）	Silky 29/29 (Green) Silky 33/33 (Black) Silky 20/20 (Brawn) Silky 55/55 (Red) 状況に合わせていろいろな貼り合わせをしてよい	
ワイヤー WIRE	＃26白地巻きワイヤー ＃26 White covered wire		
こて IRON	三筋ごて Three-lined iron		

■まじょまじょバラ　ピンクバージョン　Majo-Majo Rose
　□写真（PHOTO）P11　□型紙（PATTERN）P64

花弁(PETAL)	葉・がく (LEAF・SEPAL)	その他(MISC)
ラビアン23／シルキー23／ラビアン23 Lavien 23／Silky 23／Lavien 23	アートサテン29／シルキー29 Art Satin 29／Silky 29	
ステム〜シルキー29 Stem〜Silky 29	＃26白地巻きワイヤー ＃26 White covered wire	
ひねり Twist by hands バラ芯（小）コットン Rose core small Cotton	三筋ごて、シルキー側から 3枚葉、5枚葉 Three-lined iron from Silky side Three-leaf set, Five-leaf set	

■ まじょまじょバラ　ブルーバージョン
Majo-Majo Rose
□写真（PHOTO）P37　□型紙（PATTERN）P64

	花弁(PETAL)	葉・がく(LEAF・SEPAL)
リボン RIBBON	ラビアン10／シルキー32／ラビアン10 Lavien 10／Silky 32／Lavien 10	シルキー32／32 Silky 32／32
ワイヤー WIRE	ステム～シルキー32 Stem～Silky 32	#26白地巻きワイヤー #26 White covered wire
こて IRON	ひねり Twist by hands バラ芯（小） コットン Rose core small Cotton	3枚葉、5枚葉 Twist by hands Three-leaf set, Five-leaf set

■ まじょまじょバラ　レッドバージョン
Majo-Majo Rose
□写真（PHOTO）P17　□型紙（PATTERN）P64

	花弁(PETAL)	葉・がく(LEAF・SEPAL)
リボン RIBBON	ラビアン16／シルキー58／ラビアン16 Lavien 16／Silky 58／Lavien 16	シルキー58／ラビアン16 Silky 58／Lavien 16
ワイヤー WIRE	ステム～シルキー 58 Stem～Silky 58	#26白地巻きワイヤー #26 White covered wire
こて IRON	バラ芯（小） コットン Rose core small Cotton	三筋ごて 3枚葉、5枚葉 Three-lined iron Three-leaf set, Five-leaf set

■ 赤のチューリップ　Turip in Red　□写真（PHOTO）P3　□型紙（PATTERN）P66

	花弁(PETAL)	茎(STEM)	花芯(CORE)	その他(MISC)
リボン RIBBON	ラビアン16／シルキー16／シルキー26 Lavien16／Silky16／Silky16	シルキー33 Silky33	ゆりペップ6本 Lily Stamens 6 pieces	
ワイヤー WIRE	#24白地巻ワイヤー #White Covered		シルキー16で巻く Wrap stamen with silky16	
こて IRON	ひねり Twist by hand	三筋ごて シルキー側から Three lined iron from Silky side		

■ ダリア　Dahlia　□写真（PHOTO）P13　□型紙（PATTERN）P73

	花弁(PETAL)	茎(STEM)	がく(SEPAL)	花芯(CORE)	その他(MISC)
リボン RIBBON	ラビアン33／アートサテン16／ シルキー16／シルキー33 Lavien33／Art Satin16／Silky16／Silky33	シルキー16,33 Silky 16,33	シルキー16／33 Silky 16／33	黒のフランスペップ or おたふくペップ 5本シルキー33で巻く 5本シルキー16で巻く Black France stamen or Otafuku stamens 5 Silky33 5 Silky16 Fold in Half	コットン cotton
ワイヤー WIRE	#26白地巻き1/2 #26White Covered1/2	シルキー16で先に巻いてからシルキー33で巻く Roll stem with Silky 16 first and then Silky33			
こて IRON	筋ごて、ラビアン側から Knife shaped iron from Lavien side			ひねり Twist by hand	
MEMO	筋ごてはエッジの部分を型紙に沿う様に Stroke from top to down using Knife-shaped iron				

材料　MATERIAL

■フラワーマム　Flower Mum　□写真（PHOTO）P15　□型紙（PATTERN）P78

	花弁(PETAL)	がく(SEPAL)	花芯(CORE)	茎(STEM)	その他(MISC)
リボン RIBBON	ラビアン03／シルキー02／シルキー03 Lavien 03／Silky02／Silky02	アートサテン29／シルキー05 Art Satin 29／Silky 05	コットンバルーア04 バラペップ（ベージュ） Cotton Velour 04 Rose stamen	アートサテン29 Art Satin 29	花弁A→B→C→Dの順に花芯のまわりに内向けで。 花芯A→Bの順で＃22をいれながら。 その周りにバラペップをつける Petal A→B→C→D Place around the core Flower core A→B, with #22 wires, and then Place Rose stamens around the core
ワイヤー WIRE	＃28白地巻き1/3 #28White covered 1/3		＃22白地巻きワイヤー #22 White covered		
こて IRON	三筋ごて、ラビアン側から Three-line iron from Lavien side	三筋ごて、シルキー側から Three-line iron from Silky side			

■ホワイトローズ　White Rose　□写真（PHOTO）P15　□型紙（PATTERN）P78

	花弁(PETAL)	葉(LEAF)	茎(STEM)	がく(SEPAL)	その他(MISC)
リボン RIBBON	アートサテン01／シルキー01／ オーガンジー01 Art Stin 01／Silky01／Organdy01	コットンバルーア41／ オーガンジー05 Cotton Velour 41／ Organdy05	シルキー29（全体） 葉のステムはオーガンジー05で Silky29 Organdy05 for stem	シルキー29／29 Silky29／29	コットン、クリーム色イバラペップ15半分 花弁　アートサテン表側にボンド貼る 葉　コットンバルーア表側にオーガンジー貼る Cotton, #30 Wire Ibara Stamens（cream color）15 Petal：glue to Art Satin front Leaf：glue to Cotton Velour
ワイヤー WIRE	＃28白地巻き1/2 花弁A,Bは7枚 花弁Cは10枚 花弁Dは15枚／ワイヤー #28White Petal A,B 7 Petal C 10 Petal D 15 with wire	＃26白地巻き1/2 3枚葉、5枚葉 #26White covered Three-leaf set Five- leaf set			
こて IRON	弁ごて（大） 右半分エッジに沿って 返して左半分エッジ No-lined（Large）from right side flip over then left side	三筋ごて コットンバルーア側から 斜めに中心に向かい 返してワイヤー下から Three-lined from cotton side outer edges to center	三筋ごて シルキー側から Three lined iron from Silky side	ひねり Twisted by hand	

■まじょの小花　Majo-small Flower　□写真（PHOTO）P24　□型紙（PATTERN）P65

	花弁(PETAL)	葉(LEAF)	茎(STEM)	花芯(CORE)	その他(MISC)
リボン RIBBON	コットンバルーア01／ アートサテン02,14,01,63 Cotton Velour 01／ Satin 02,14,01,63	コットンバルーア01／アートサテン02,14,01,63 花弁と同じ貼り合わせ Cotton Velour 01／Satin 02,14, 01,63 Same lamination as petal	シルキー01 Silky 01	ツートンペップ Two-tone stamen	花3つを最短につけて束ね、葉を4枚つける これを3本作り、3枚になる様に組む 残りの葉を足しシルキー01で巻きおろす Bundle 3 flowers with 4 leaves Make 3 branches and set like 3 leaves Place remains Leaves with Silky 01
ワイヤー WIRE		＃26白地巻き1/2 #26White covered 1/2			
こて IRON	すずらんごて、アートサテン側から Suzuran iron, from Satin	三筋ごて アートサテン側から Three-lined iron from Satin			

■まじょのグラジオラス　gladiolus　□写真（PHOTO）P26　□型紙（PATTERN）P65

	花弁（PETAL）	葉（LEAF）	茎（STEM）	がく（SEPAL）	花芯（CORE）	その他（MISC）
リボン RIBBON	シルキーオンブレー17／17 シルキー55／58 Silky Ombre17／17 Silky 55／58	ラビアン33／シルキー17／シルキー33 Lavien 33／Silky 17／Silky 33	シルキー33 silky33 シルキー33／98 Silky 33／98	シルキー33／98 Silky 33／98	ガラスペップ（白）6本 Glass stamen 6 pieces	花弁6枚を花芯のまわりに付ける がくで根元をくるむ 残りのがく2枚をガーランドし、花をつける ステムは斜め巻きをした後に、くるむように付ける 葉は6枚を束ねてアレンジに使う。 または花茎の下につけても良い Place 6 petals around the core Wrap the bottom with Sepal ribbon Use 2 remain Sepal to set and place flowers After use stem tape, then Wrap the stem with sepal ribbon
ワイヤー WIRE	＃26白地巻き1/2 ＃26White covered 1/2	＃22白地巻き ＃22White covered				
こて IRON	ひねり Twist by hand	ひねり Twisted by hand		ひねり Twisted by hand		

■ぼたん　Peony　□写真（PHOTO）P30　□型紙（PATTERN）P75

	花弁（PETAL）	葉（LEAF）	茎（STEM）	がく（SEPAL）	花芯（CORE）	その他（MISC）
リボン RIBBON	シルキーオンブレ14／23 Silky Ombre 14／23	オーガンジー05／シルキー29 Organdy 05／Silky 29	シルキー29 Silky 29	シルキー05／29 Silky 05／29	オーガンジー05 素ボール10mm Organdy 05 Styrofoam bal 10mm	
ワイヤー WIRE	＃26白地巻き ＃26White covered	＃26白地巻き 3枚葉に組む ＃26White covered Three-leaf set		＃26白地巻き1/2 ＃26white covered	イバラペップ（黄） Rose stamen（yellow）	
こて IRON	弁ごて No-lined iron	三筋ごて Three -lined iron		三筋ごて Three -lined iron		

■めだかの葉っぱ　Medaka leaf　□写真（PHOTO）P30　□型紙（PATTERN）P★

	葉（LEAF）	茎（STEM）	その他（MISC）
リボン RIBBON	シルキー17／18 Silky 17／18	シルキー17 Silky 17	
ワイヤー WIRE	＃28白地巻き ＃28 White Covered		
こて IRON	ひねり Twisted by hand		

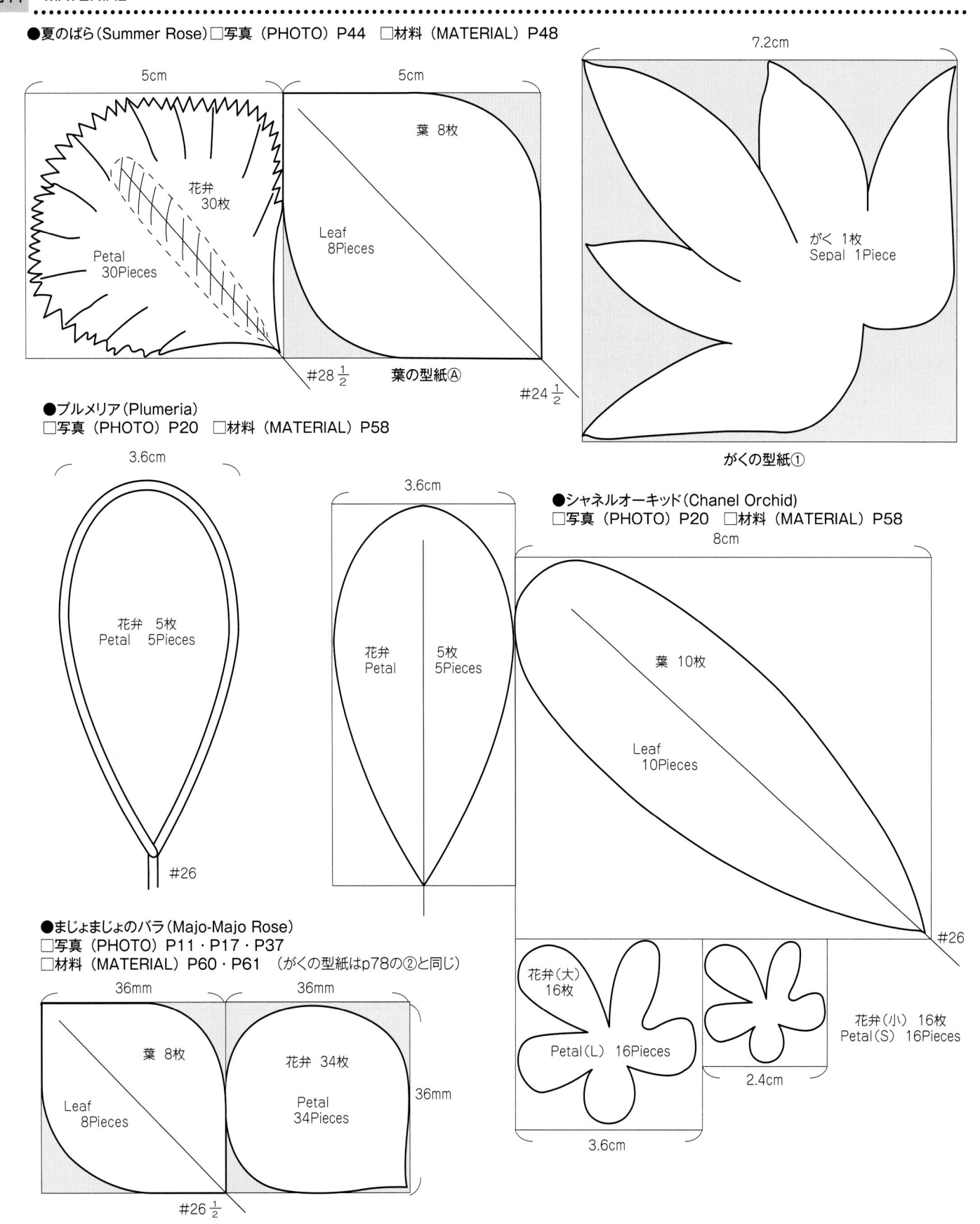

材料　MATERIAL

●夏のばら(Summer Rose) □写真（PHOTO）P44　□材料（MATERIAL）P48

5cm

花弁 30枚
Petal 30Pieces

5cm

葉 8枚
Leaf 8Pieces

#28 ½　葉の型紙Ⓐ

7.2cm

がく 1枚
Sepal 1Piece

#24 ½

がくの型紙①

●プルメリア(Plumeria)
□写真（PHOTO）P20　□材料（MATERIAL）P58

3.6cm

花弁　5枚
Petal　5Pieces

3.6cm

花弁　5枚
Petal　5Pieces

#26

●シャネルオーキッド(Chanel Orchid)
□写真（PHOTO）P20　□材料（MATERIAL）P58

8cm

葉 10枚
Leaf 10Pieces

#26

花弁(大) 16枚
Petal(L) 16Pieces

3.6cm

花弁(小) 16枚
Petal(S) 16Pieces

2.4cm

●まじょまじょのバラ(Majo-Majo Rose)
□写真（PHOTO）P11・P17・P37
□材料（MATERIAL）P60・P61　（がくの型紙はp78の②と同じ）

36mm

葉 8枚
Leaf 8Pieces

36mm

花弁 34枚
Petal 34Pieces

36mm

#26 ½

● 小さい菊の花（Small Daisy）
□ 写真（PHOTO）P41　□ 材料（MATERIAL）P48

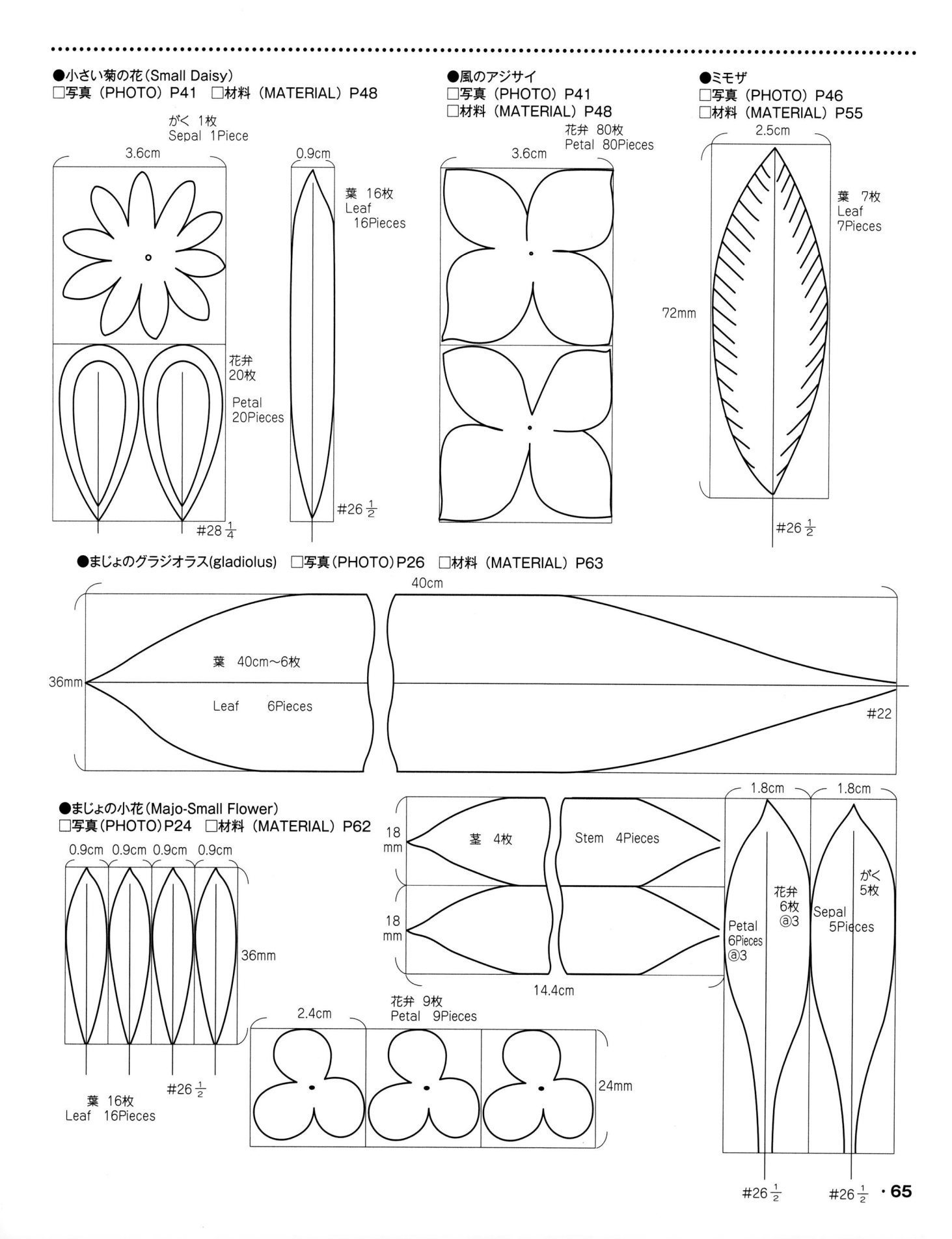

がく 1枚
Sepal 1Piece
3.6cm
0.9cm
葉 16枚
Leaf 16Pieces
花弁 20枚
Petal 20Pieces
#28 $\frac{1}{4}$
#26 $\frac{1}{2}$

● 風のアジサイ
□ 写真（PHOTO）P41
□ 材料（MATERIAL）P48

花弁 80枚
Petal 80Pieces
3.6cm

● ミモザ
□ 写真（PHOTO）P46
□ 材料（MATERIAL）P55

2.5cm
葉 7枚
Leaf 7Pieces
72mm
#26 $\frac{1}{2}$

● まじょのグラジオラス(gladiolus)　□ 写真（PHOTO）P26　□ 材料（MATERIAL）P63

40cm
36mm
葉 40cm〜6枚
Leaf 6Pieces
#22

● まじょの小花（Majo-Small Flower）
□ 写真（PHOTO）P24　□ 材料（MATERIAL）P62

0.9cm 0.9cm 0.9cm 0.9cm
36mm
葉 16枚
Leaf 16Pieces
#26 $\frac{1}{2}$

18mm
茎 4枚
Stem 4Pieces
18mm
14.4cm

2.4cm
花弁 9枚
Petal 9Pieces
24mm

1.8cm　1.8cm
花弁 6枚 @3
Petal 6Pieces @3
がく 5枚
Sepal 5Pieces
#26 $\frac{1}{2}$　#26 $\frac{1}{2}$

・65

型紙　PATTERN

●水色の涙(Blue Tears)　□写真(PHOTO)P36　□材料(MATERIAL)P49

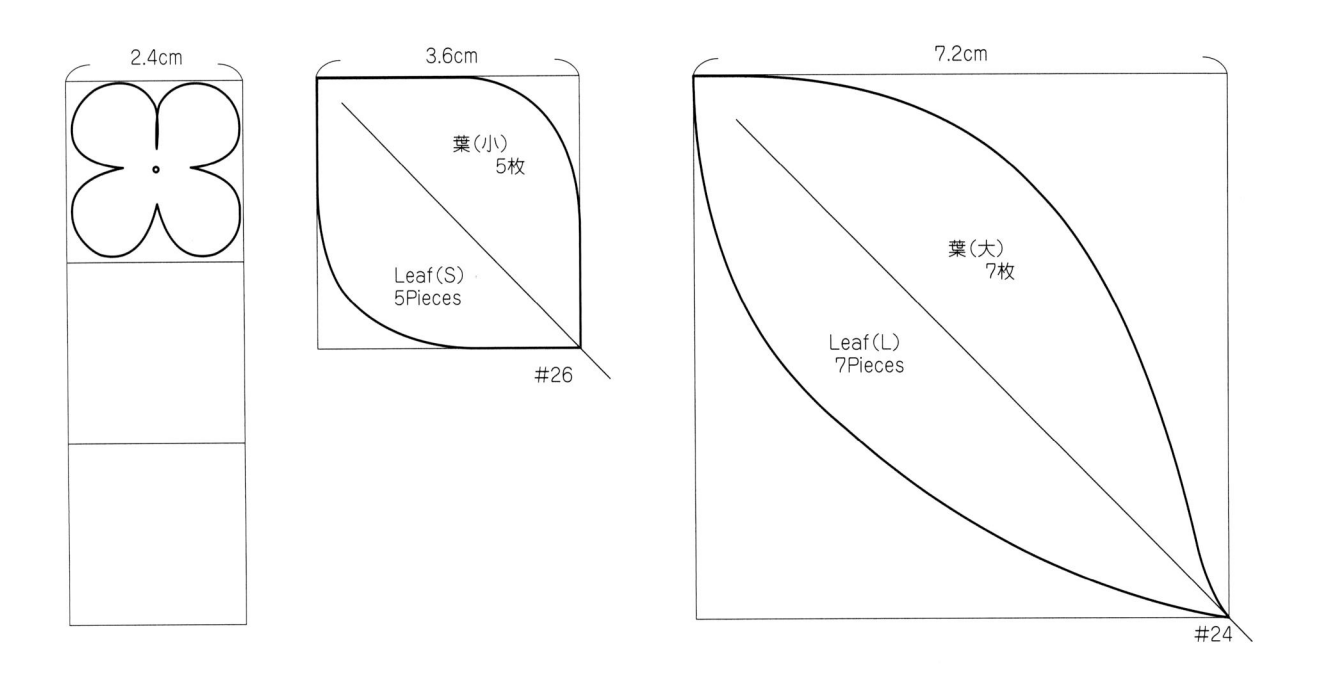

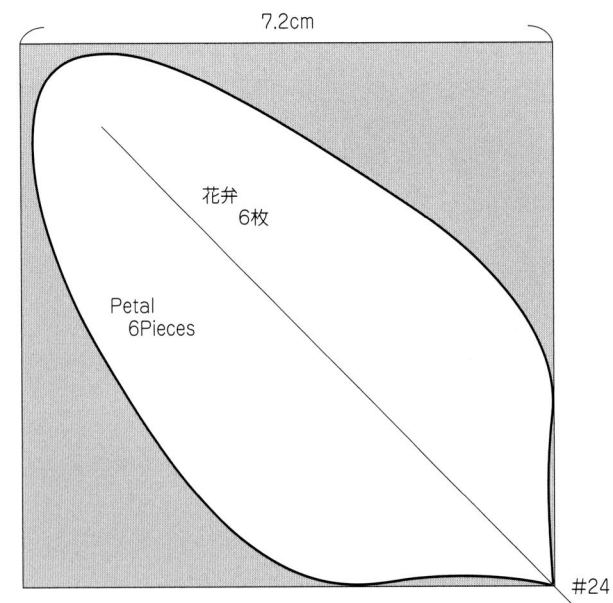

2.4cm

3.6cm

葉(小)
5枚

Leaf(S)
5Pieces

#26

7.2cm

葉(大)
7枚

Leaf(L)
7Pieces

#24

●赤のチューリップ(Tulip in Red)
□写真(PHOTO)P3　□材料(MATERIAL)P61

7.2cm

花弁
6枚

Petal
6Pieces

#24

66・

● 火の鳥 (Fire bird)　□写真（PHOTO）P16　□材料（MATERIAL）P49

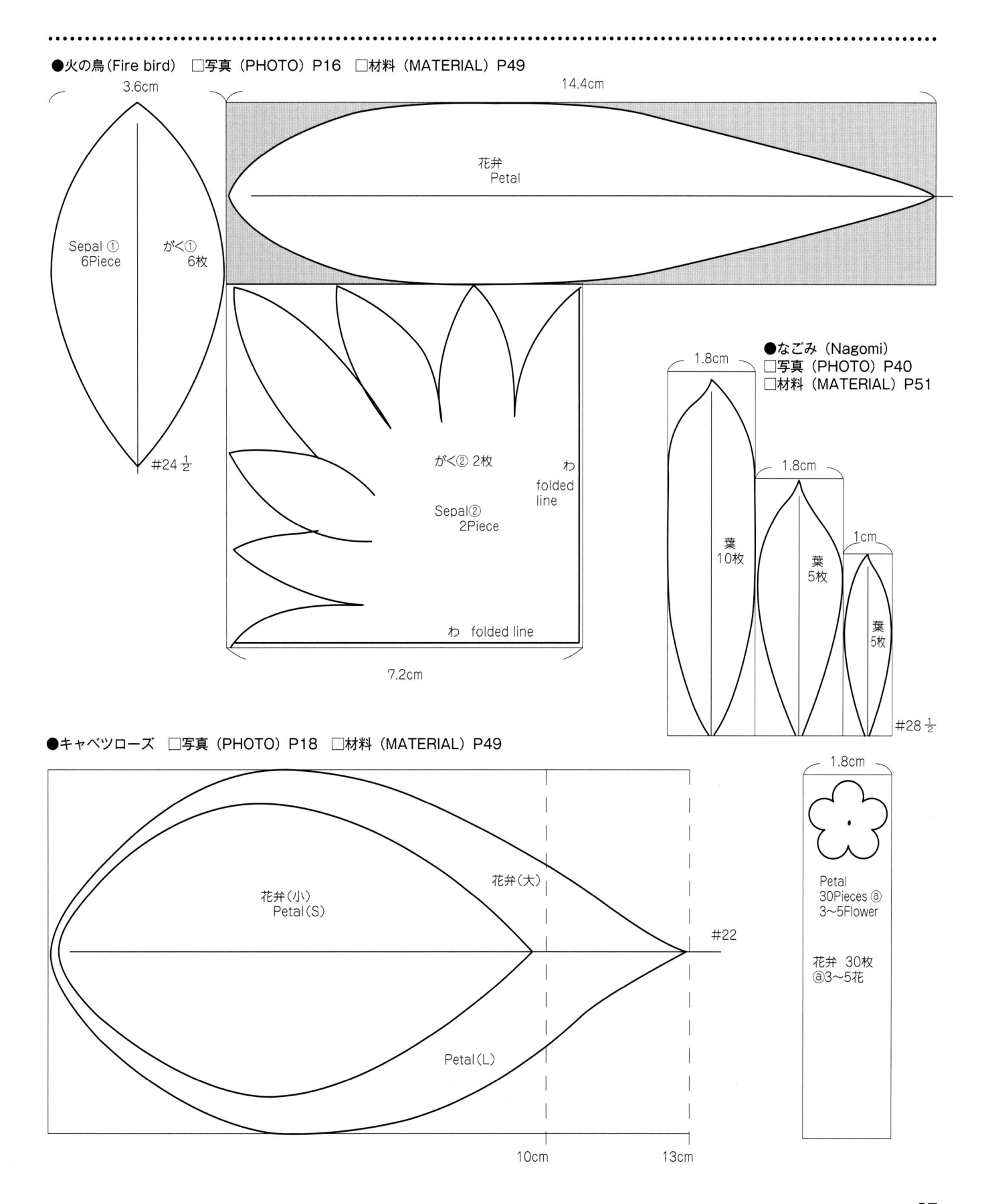

3.6cm　　　14.4cm

花弁
Petal

Sepal ①
6Piece

がく①
6枚

#24 1/2

がく② 2枚
Sepal ②
2Piece

わ folded line
わ folded line

7.2cm

● なごみ（Nagomi）
□写真（PHOTO）P40
□材料（MATERIAL）P51

1.8cm　1.8cm　1cm

葉 10枚　葉 5枚　葉 5枚

#28 1/2

● キャベツローズ　□写真（PHOTO）P18　□材料（MATERIAL）P49

花弁(小)
Petal(S)

花弁(大)
Petal(L)

#22

10cm　13cm

1.8cm

Petal
30Pieces @
3～5Flower

花弁 30枚
@3～5花

· 67

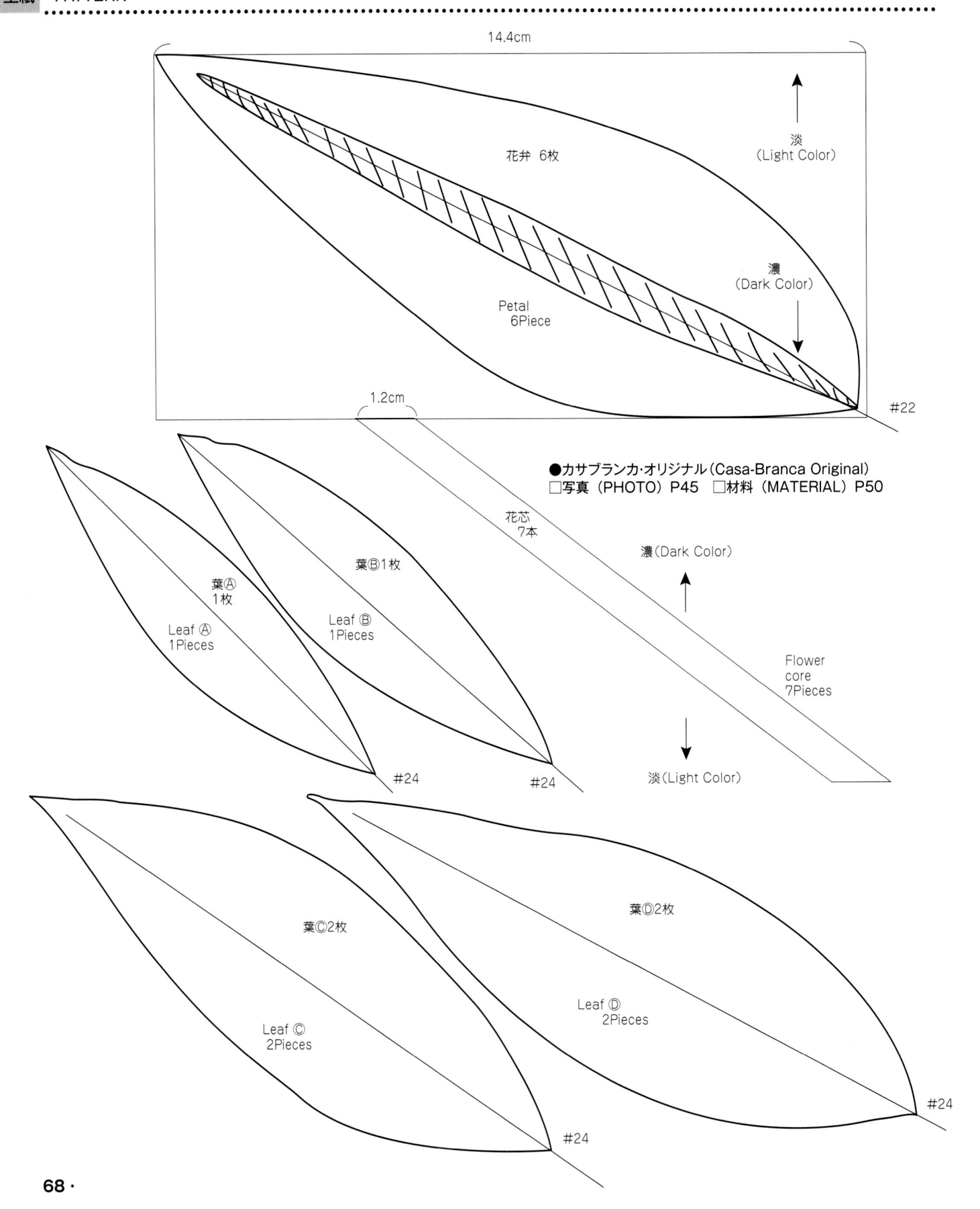

型紙 PATTERN

14.4cm

花弁 6枚
Petal 6Piece

淡 (Light Color)
濃 (Dark Color)

#22

1.2cm

●カサブランカ・オリジナル (Casa-Branca Original)
□写真 (PHOTO) P45 □材料 (MATERIAL) P50

葉Ⓐ 1枚
Leaf Ⓐ 1Pieces

葉Ⓑ 1枚
Leaf Ⓑ 1Pieces

#24   #24

花芯 7本
Flower core 7Pieces

濃 (Dark Color)
淡 (Light Color)

葉Ⓒ 2枚
Leaf Ⓒ 2Pieces

葉Ⓓ 2枚
Leaf Ⓓ 2Pieces

#24   #24

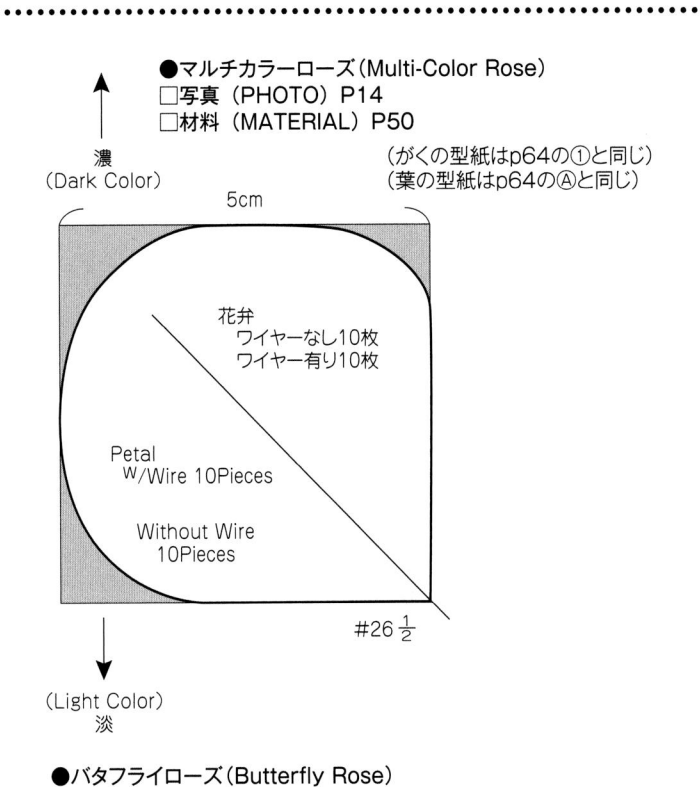

● マルチカラーローズ（Multi-Color Rose）
□ 写真（PHOTO）P14
□ 材料（MATERIAL）P50

↑ 濃 (Dark Color)

（がくの型紙はp64の①と同じ）
（葉の型紙はp64のⒶと同じ）

5cm

花弁
ワイヤーなし10枚
ワイヤー有り10枚

Petal
W/Wire 10Pieces

Without Wire
10Pieces

#26 ½

↓ (Light Color) 淡

● まじょのどくいちご
□ 写真（PHOTO）P5・P17・P40
□ 材料（MATERIAL）P50

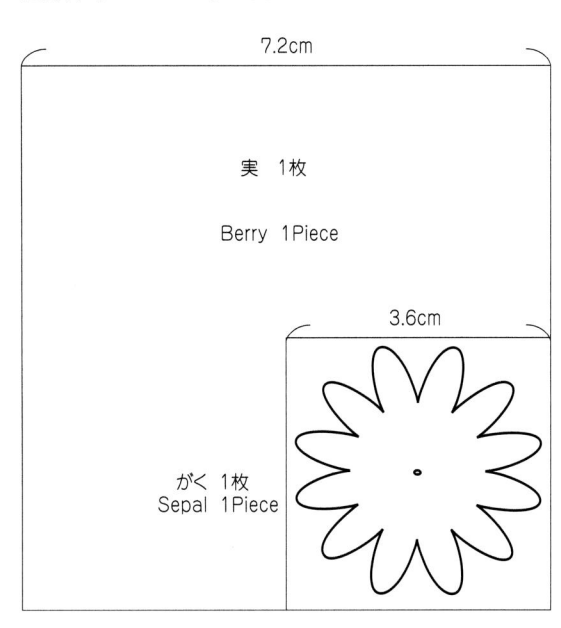

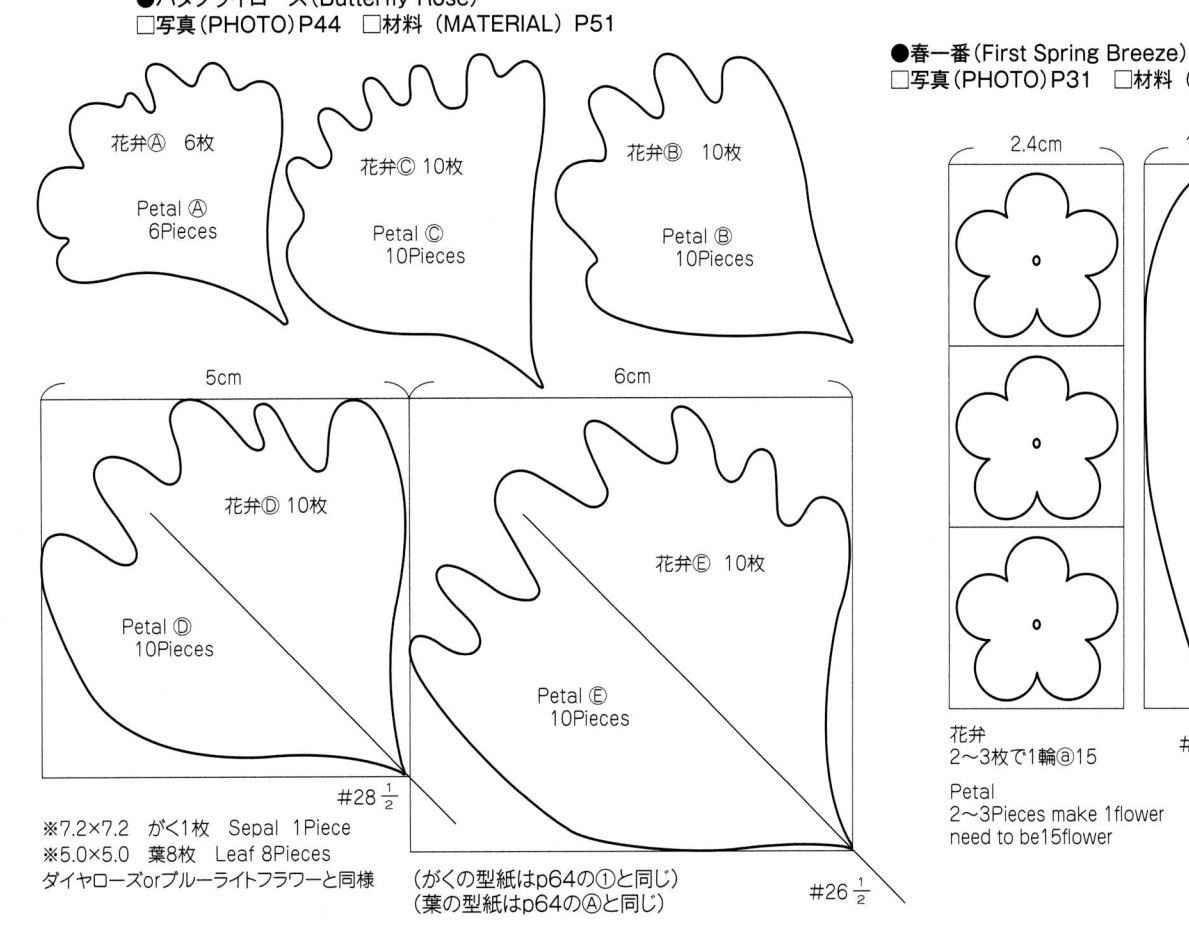

7.2cm

実　1枚
Berry　1Piece

3.6cm

がく　1枚
Sepal　1Piece

● バタフライローズ（Butterfly Rose）
□ 写真（PHOTO）P44　□ 材料（MATERIAL）P51

花弁Ⓐ　6枚
Petal Ⓐ
6Pieces

花弁Ⓒ　10枚
Petal Ⓒ
10Pieces

花弁Ⓑ　10枚
Petal Ⓑ
10Pieces

5cm

花弁Ⓓ　10枚
Petal Ⓓ
10Pieces

#28 ½

6cm

花弁Ⓔ　10枚
Petal Ⓔ
10Pieces

（がくの型紙はp64の①と同じ）
（葉の型紙はp64のⒶと同じ）

#26 ½

※7.2×7.2　がく1枚　Sepal 1Piece
※5.0×5.0　葉8枚　Leaf 8Pieces
ダイヤローズorブルーライトフラワーと同様

● 春一番（First Spring Breeze）
□ 写真（PHOTO）P31　□ 材料（MATERIAL）P52

2.4cm　　1.8cm

#26 ½

葉
10枚
Leaf
10Pieces

#26 ½

花弁
2〜3枚で1輪＠15

Petal
2〜3Pieces make 1flower
need to be15flower

型紙 PATTERN

●サンバドロップ (Samba Drop)
□写真（PHOTO）P28　□材料（MATERIAL）P51

2.4cm

1.8cm

葉 8枚
Leaf 8Pieces

がく 18枚
Sepal 18Piece

#26 1/2

3.6cm

実
Berry

●マルチカラーフラワー（Multi Color Flower）
□写真（PHOTO）P7
□材料（MATERIAL）P52

1cm

（がくの型紙はp64の①と同じ）
（葉の型紙はp64のⒶと同じ）

花弁 5～60枚
Petal 5～60Pieces

●星の枝 (Star Branch)
□写真（PHOTO）P44
□材料（MATERIAL）P56

5cm

花弁 7枚

50mm

星の数

Petal 7Pieces

#26 wire

●フラワーカトリーヌ (Flower Catherine)
□写真（PHOTO）P4　□材料（MATERIAL）P52

3.6cm

花弁Ⓐ 3枚
PetalⒶ 3Pieces

3.6cm

花弁Ⓑ 3枚
PetalⒷ 3Pieces

#26 1/3

3.6cm

花弁Ⓒ 3枚
PetalⒸ 3Pieces

3.6cm

花弁Ⓓ 5枚
PetalⒹ 5Pieces

●ポップコーン (Popcorn)
□写真（PHOTO）P46
□材料（MATERIAL）P56

4cm

花弁 30枚
Petal 30Pieces

ポップコーン

72mm

●赤ちゃんの小枝
(Baby Hand Branch)
□写真（PHOTO）P36
□材料（MATERIAL）P53

18mm

葉 20枚
Leaf 20Pieces

わ
(Folded line)

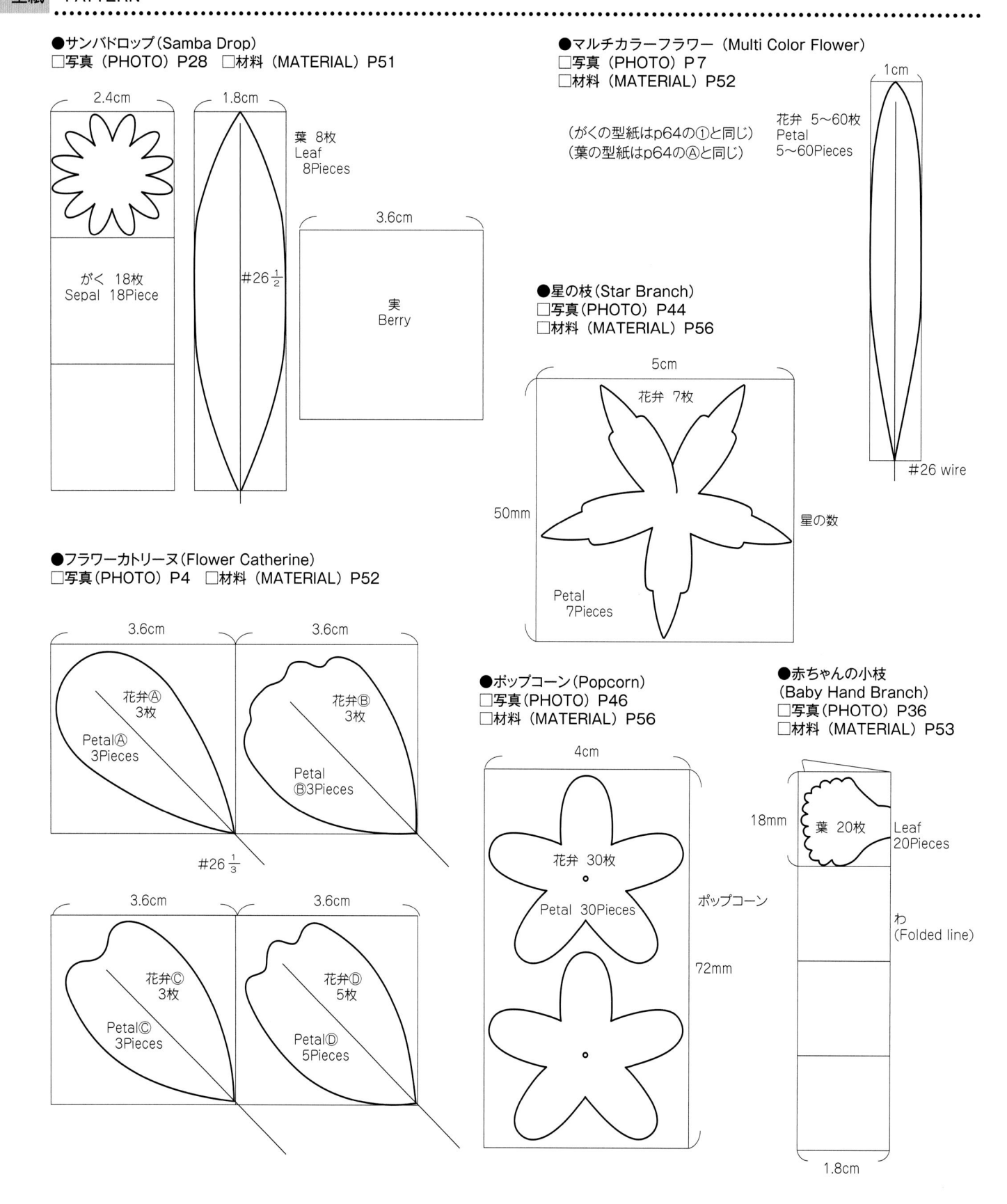

1.8cm

● ダイヤローズ(Diamond Rose)
  □ 写真(PHOTO) P27・P32
  □ 材料(MATERIAL) P53

(がくの型紙はp64の①と同じ)
(葉の型紙はp64のⒶと同じ)

3.6cm
24mm
3 Pieces 3枚

45mm
4 Pieces 4枚

36mm
6 Pieces 6枚

0.9cm
16枚 16 Pieces
16枚 16 Pieces

1.8cm
16枚 16 Pieces

1.8cm
16枚 16 Pieces
65mm
60mm
50mm

1.8cm
20枚 20 Pieces
72mm

#28 ½

● オーガンジーのバラ(Organdy Rose)
  □ 写真(PHOTO) P36・P47 □ 材料(MATERIAL) P54

3.6cm
花弁 50枚 Petal 50Pieces

葉 8枚 Leaf 8Pieces
36mm
#26 ½

※P56の本ガンジーローズと同じ
花弁 → 本ガンジー 04
         Organdy 04

6cm
がく 1枚 Sepal 1Piece
60mm

がくの型紙②

● マーガレット(Marguerite)
  □ 写真(PHOTO) P36 □ 材料(MATERIAL) P54

10cm
9mm
わ(Folded Line)

花芯(Flower Core)

シルキー04 (Silky 04) 〜4枚 (4Pieces)
シルキー29 (Silky 29) 〜1枚 (1Pieces)

0.8 0.8
花弁 36枚 Petal 36Pieces
50mm
#28 ⅓

3.6cm
葉 5枚 Leaf 5Pieces
72mm

4cm
がく 1枚 Sepal 1Piece
40mm

#26 ½

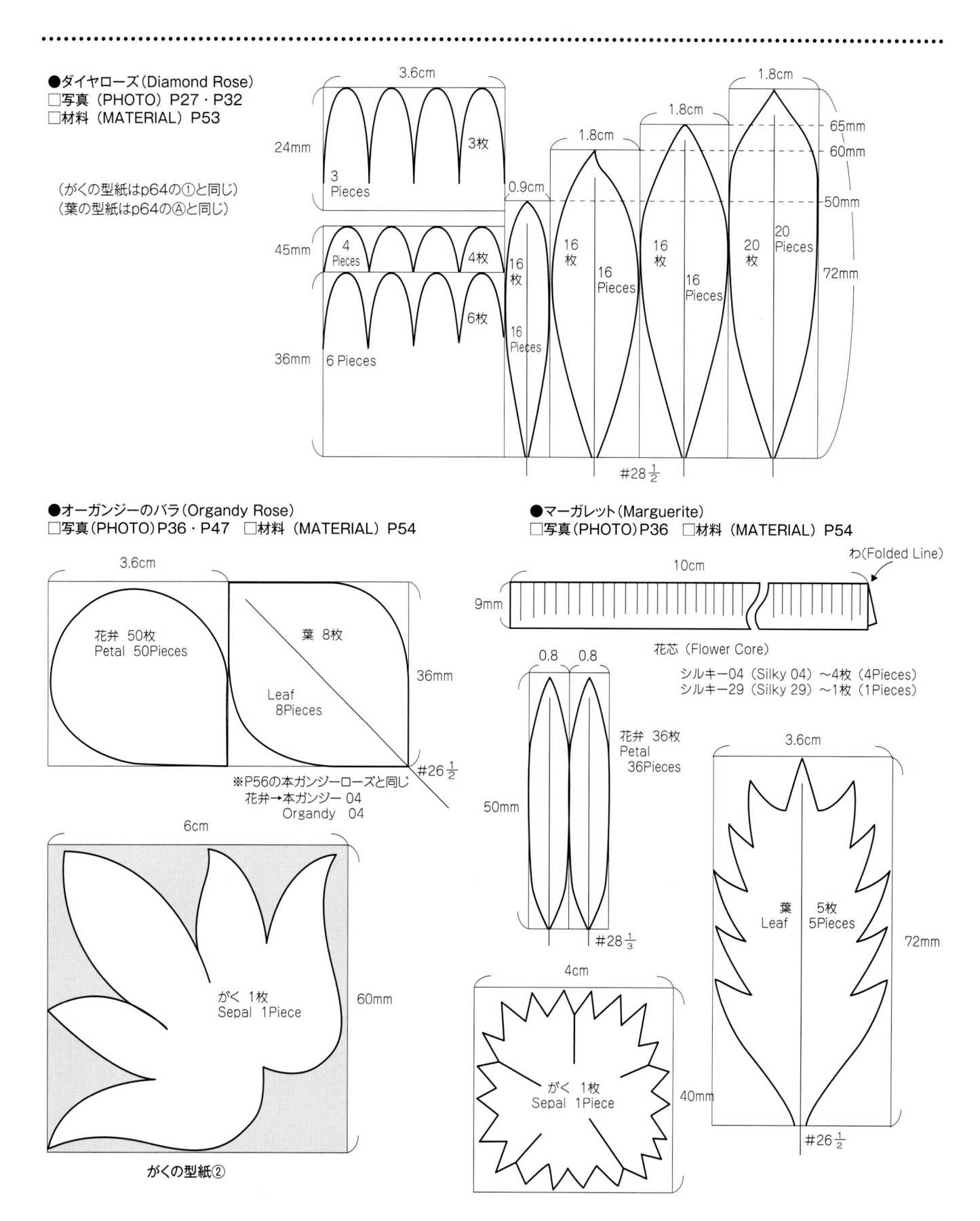

・71

型紙 PATTERN

●ブルーライトフラワー (Blue Light Flower)　□写真 (PHOTO) P6　□材料 (MATERIAL) P53

（がくの型紙はp64の①と同じ）
（葉の型紙はp64のⒶと同じ）

- 2.4cm / PetalⒶ 10Pieces / 花弁Ⓐ 10枚 / 50mm / #28 ½
- 3.6cm / PetalⒷ 10Pieces / 花弁Ⓑ 10枚 / #26 ½
- 5cm / PetalⒸ 10Pieces / 花弁Ⓒ 10枚 / #26 ½
- 7.2cm / PetalⒹ 10Pieces / 花弁Ⓓ 10枚 / 7.2mm / #26 ½
- 9cm / 72mm / PetalⒺ 10Pieces / 花弁Ⓔ 10枚 / #26 ½

●ライラック (Lilac)
□写真 (PHOTO) P10・P36
□材料 (MATERIAL) P54

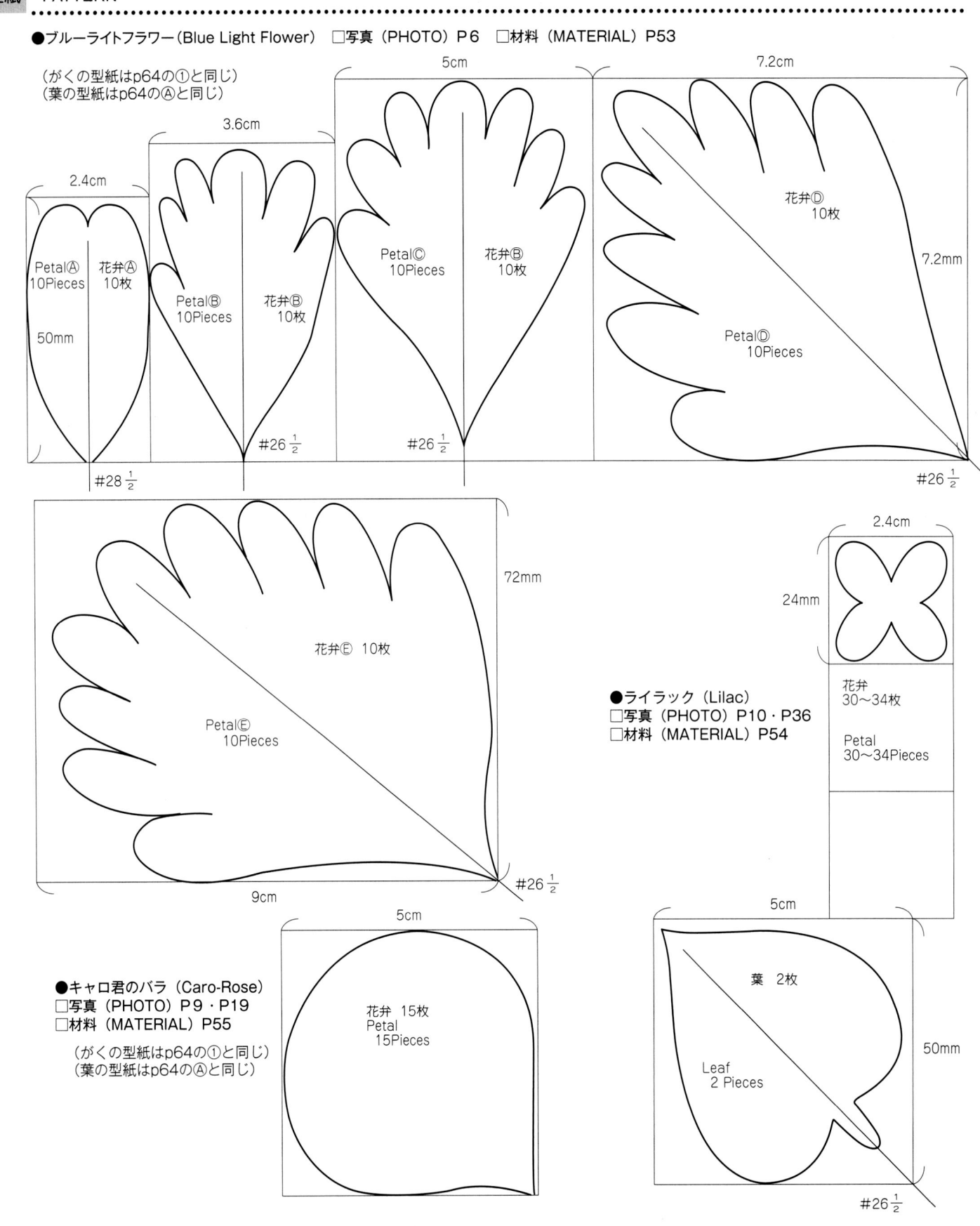

- 2.4cm / 24mm / 花弁 30〜34枚 / Petal 30〜34Pieces

●キャロ君のバラ (Caro-Rose)
□写真 (PHOTO) P9・P19
□材料 (MATERIAL) P55

（がくの型紙はp64の①と同じ）
（葉の型紙はp64のⒶと同じ）

- 5cm / 花弁 15枚 / Petal 15Pieces
- 5cm / 葉 2枚 / Leaf 2 Pieces / 50mm / #26 ½

- フリージア (Freesia) 写真(PHOTO) P36 材料(MATERIAL) P54

20cm/23cm
葉 各2枚
Leaf 2Pieces each
#24
18mm

がく 5枚
Sepal 5Piece
12mm
1.5cm

7.2cm
花弁(大) 1枚
Petal(L) 1Piece
72mm

つぼみ(大)
Bud(L) 1Piece
30mm

つぼみ(小) 1枚
Bud(S) 1Piece
2cm

花弁(小) 1枚
Petal(S) 1Piece
42mm
4cm

- ダリア (Dahlia)
写真(PHOTO) P13 材料(MATERIAL) P61
(がくの型紙はp64の①と同じ)

2.4cm 2.4cm 2.4cm
花弁 30枚
Petal 30Pieces
#26 ½

18cm
葉 2枚
Leaf 2 Pieces
50mm
72mm

花弁(小) 3枚
Petal(S) 3Pieces
5cm
#26

花弁(大) 3枚
Petal(L) 3Pieces
5cm
#26

#24

- チューリップ (Tulip)
写真(PHOTO) P10・P36
材料(MATERIAL) P55

- ベアグラス (Beargrass)
写真(PHOTO) P6・P16・P46
材料(MATERIAL) P60

24mm
24mm
#26
12本 12Pieces (20〜30cm)

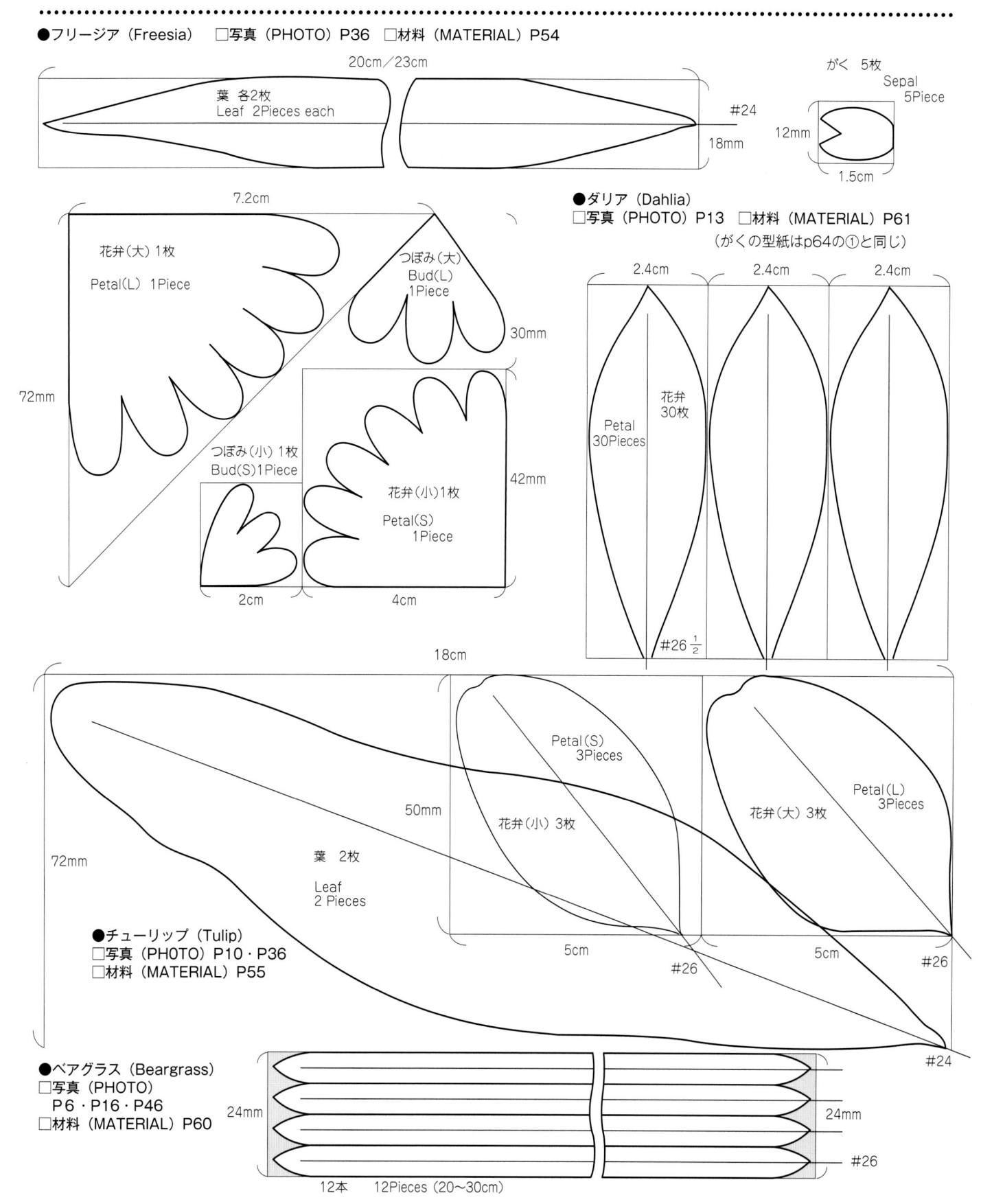

・73

型紙 PATTERN

●ガーベラ（Gerbera） □写真（PHOTO）P9・P22 □材料（MATERIAL）P55

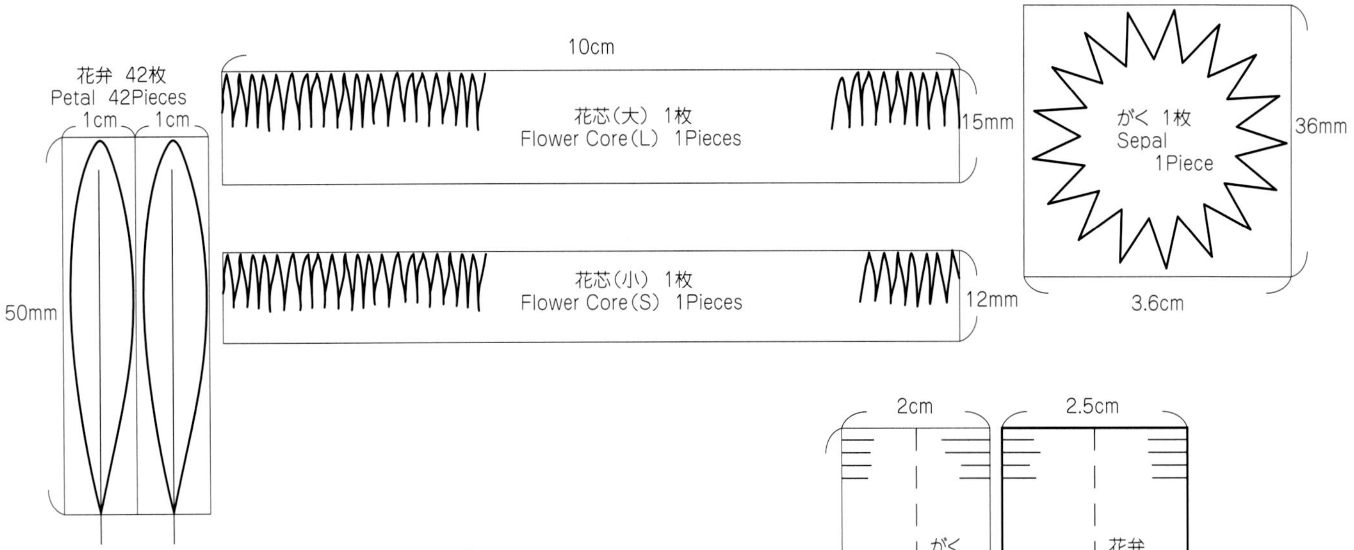

花弁 42枚
Petal 42Pieces
1cm 1cm
50mm

10cm
花芯（大） 1枚
Flower Core（L） 1Pieces
15mm

花芯（小） 1枚
Flower Core（S） 1Pieces
12mm

がく 1枚
Sepal 1Piece
36mm
3.6cm

●スターチス（Statice）
□写真（PHOTO）P46 □材料（MATERIAL）P56

15cm
18mm

茎 4枚
Stem 4Pieces

2cm
がく 4枚
わ（Folded line）
Sepal 4Pieces
72mm

2.5cm
花弁 4枚
わ（Folded line）
Petal 4Pieces

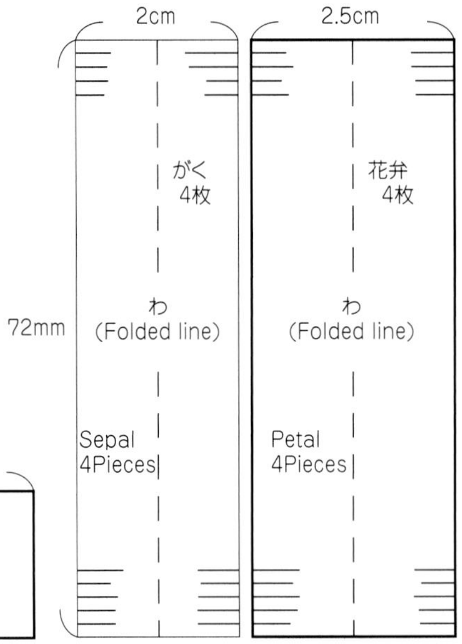

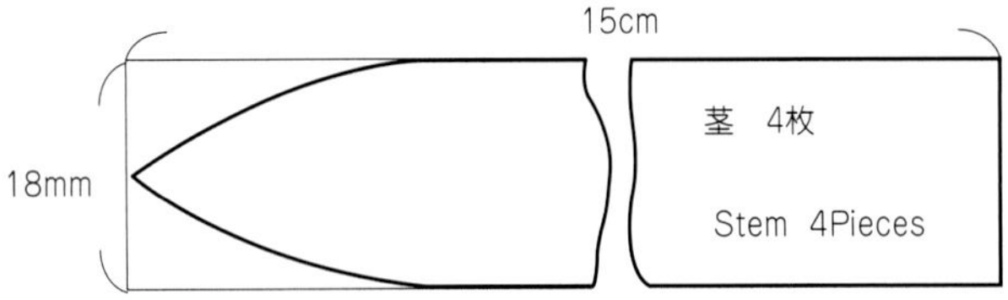

●コインリーフ（Coin Leaf）
□写真（PHOTO）P46 □材料（MATERIAL）P56

3.6cm
#28
36mm

コインリーフ 10枚
Coin Leaf 10Pieces

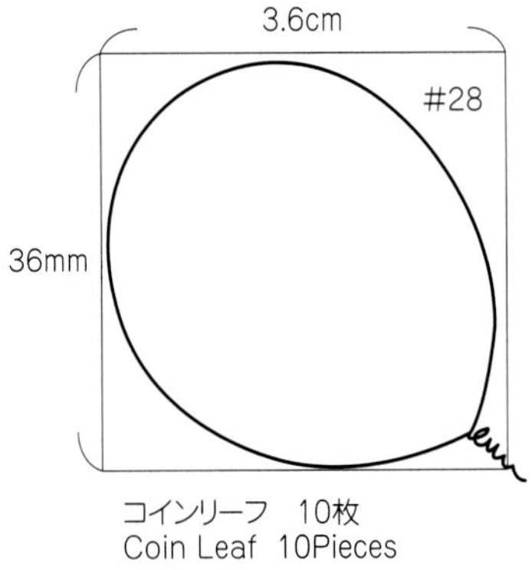

●日月潭 ●ローズホープ（Rose of Hope）
□写真（PHOTO）P35・P39
□材料（MATERIAL）P58
（がくの型紙はp71の②と同じ）

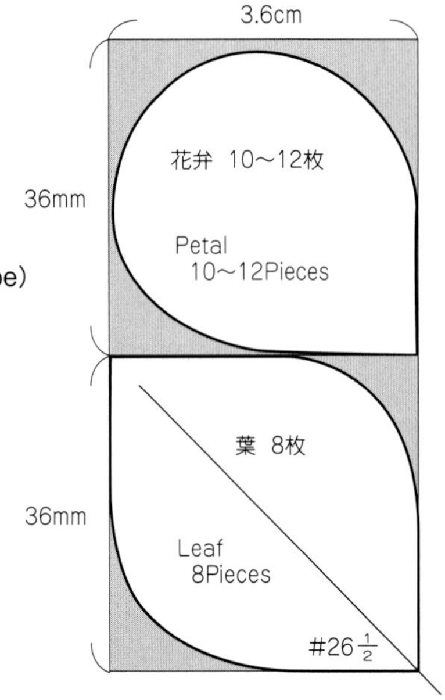

3.6cm
花弁 10～12枚
Petal 10～12Pieces
36mm

葉 8枚
Leaf 8Pieces
36mm
#26 $\frac{1}{2}$

74・

●赤いカーネーション (Red Carnation)
□写真 (PHOTO) P40 □材料 (MATERIAL) P57

7.2cm (3″)
72mm (3″)
花弁 20枚
Petal 20Pieces

4.5cm (1 4/5″)
1cm (2/5″)
60mm (2 1/3″)
がく 1枚
Sepal 1Piece
葉 8枚
Leaf 8Pieces
ワイヤー #26 wire 1/2

●ぼたん (Peony)
□写真 (PHOTO) P30
□材料 (MATERIAL) P63

5cm
50mm
がく A 1枚
Sepal Ⓐ 1Piece

6cm
葉Ⓐ 1枚
Leaf Ⓐ 1Piece
#26

8.5cm
72mm
葉Ⓑ 2枚
Leaf Ⓑ 16Pieces
#26

9cm
72mm
3.6cm
36mm
花弁(大) 10枚
Petal (L) 10Pieces
#26
花芯 3枚
Flower Core 3Pieces

6cm
花弁(小) 10枚
Petal (S) 10Pieces
#26

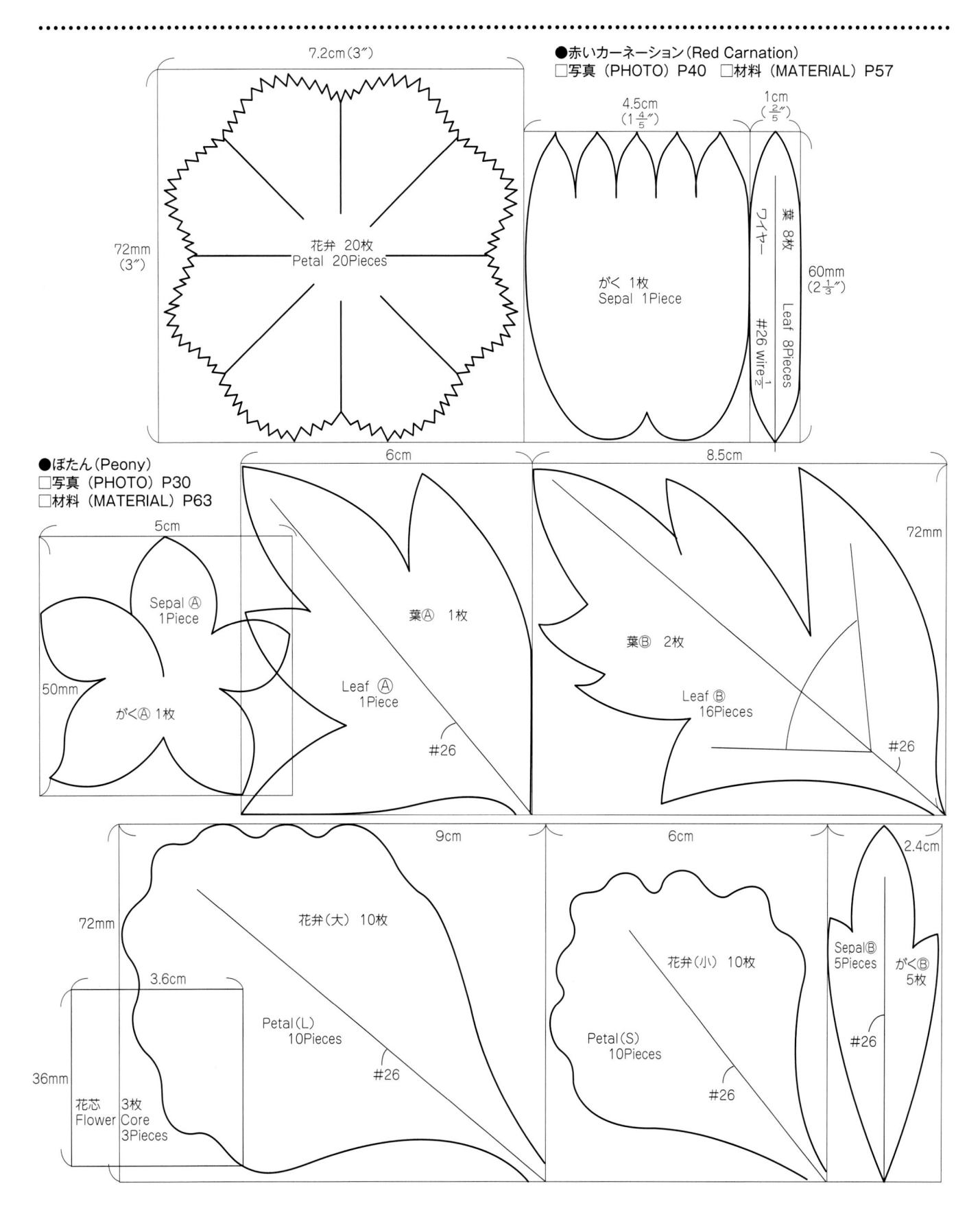

2.4cm
がくⒷ 5枚
Sepal Ⓑ 5Pieces
#26

型紙 PATTERN

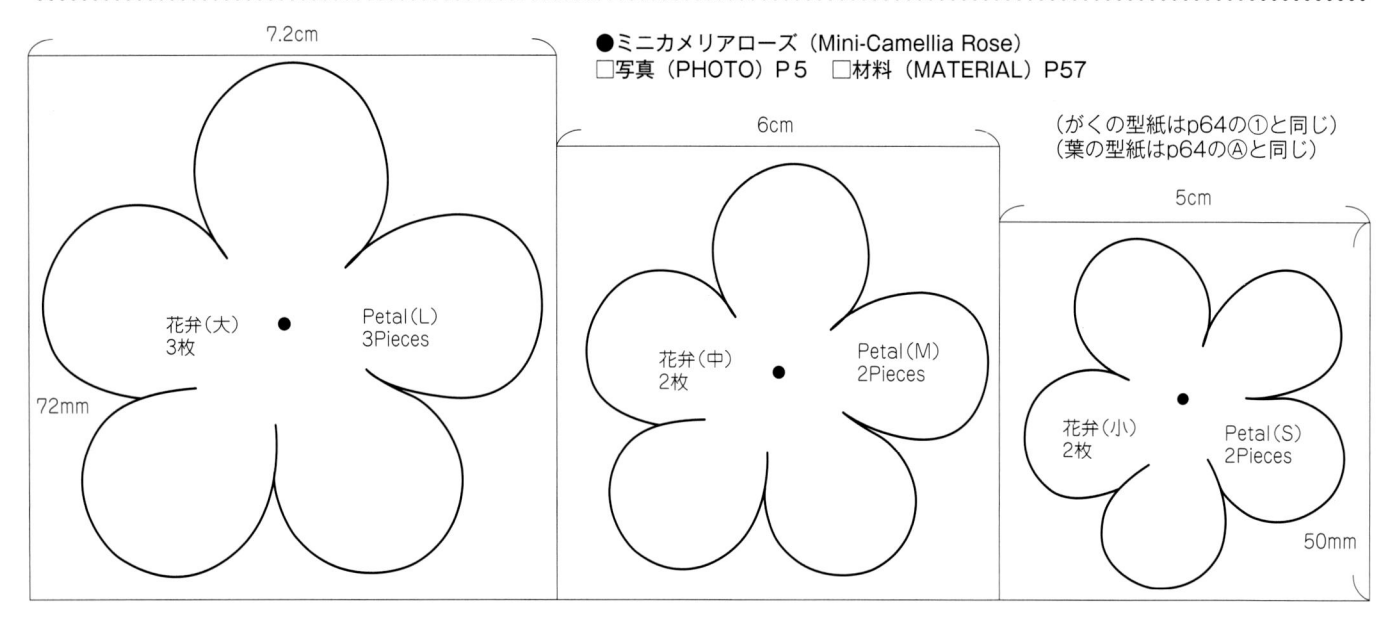

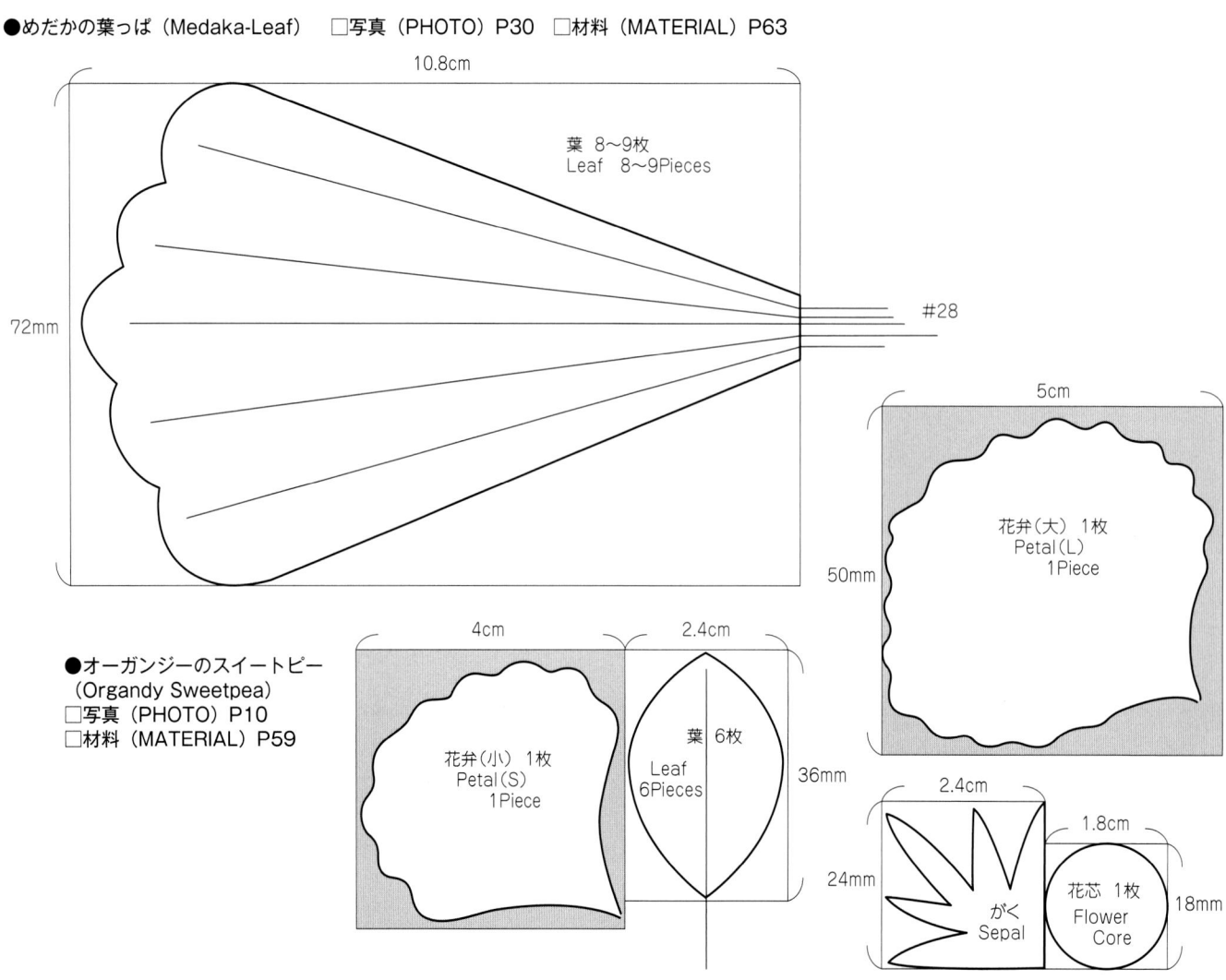

● ミニカメリアローズ (Mini-Camellia Rose)
□ 写真 (PHOTO) P5 □ 材料 (MATERIAL) P57

（がくの型紙はp64の①と同じ）
（葉の型紙はp64のⒶと同じ）

7.2cm / 72mm — 花弁（大）3枚 / Petal(L) 3Pieces
6cm — 花弁（中）2枚 / Petal(M) 2Pieces
5cm / 50mm — 花弁（小）2枚 / Petal(S) 2Pieces

● めだかの葉っぱ (Medaka-Leaf)
□ 写真 (PHOTO) P30 □ 材料 (MATERIAL) P63

10.8cm / 72mm — 葉 8〜9枚 / Leaf 8〜9Pieces #28

● オーガンジーのスイートピー
（Organdy Sweetpea）
□ 写真 (PHOTO) P10
□ 材料 (MATERIAL) P59

5cm / 50mm — 花弁（大）1枚 / Petal(L) 1Piece
4cm — 花弁（小）1枚 / Petal(S) 1Piece
2.4cm / 36mm — 葉 6枚 / Leaf 6Pieces
2.4cm / 24mm — がく / Sepal
1.8cm / 18mm — 花芯 1枚 / Flower Core

76

● カトレア (Cattleya)　□写真 (PHOTO) P20　□材料 (MATERIAL) P58

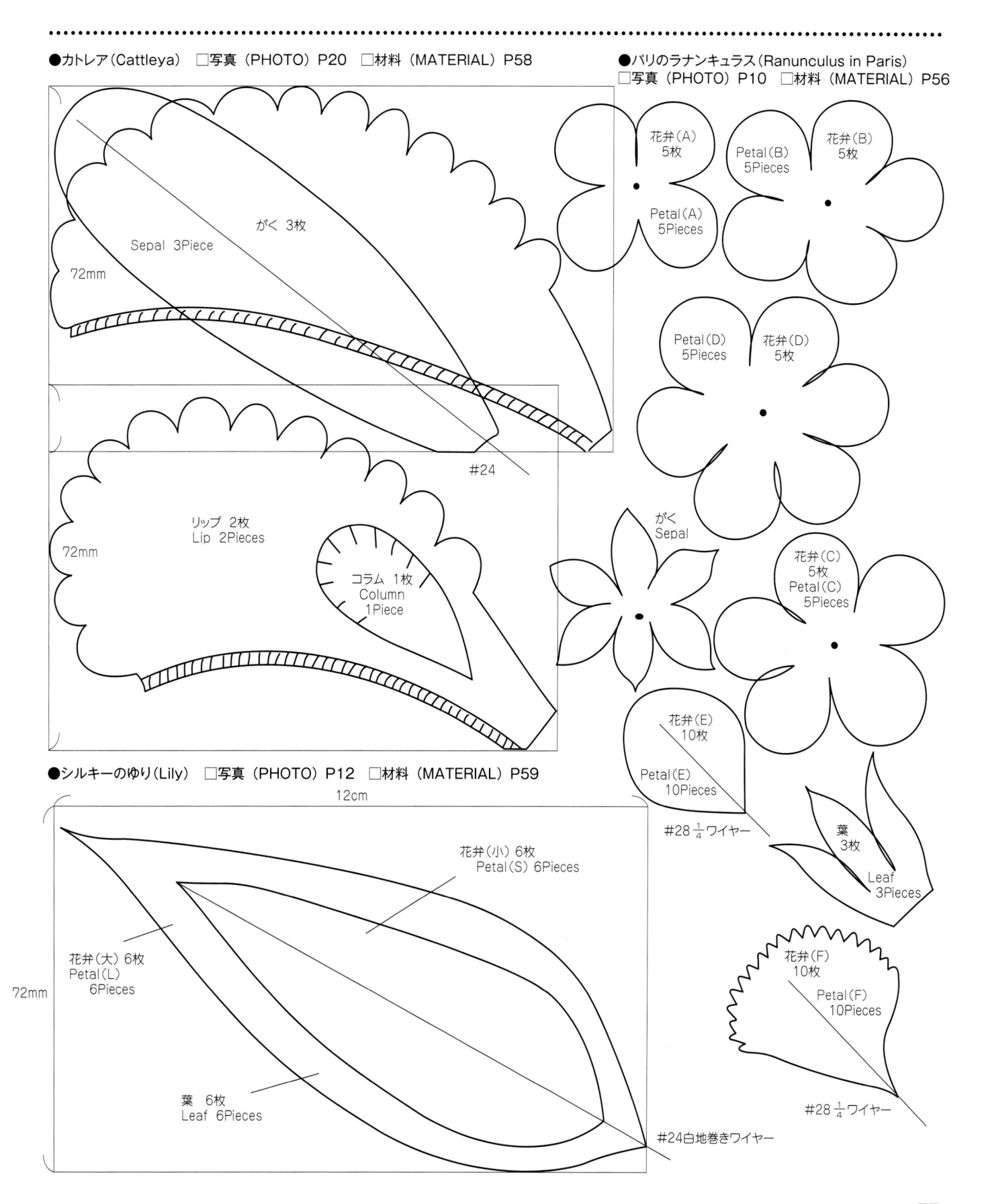

がく 3枚
Sepal 3Piece
72mm
#24

リップ 2枚
Lip 2Pieces
72mm

コラム 1枚
Column 1Piece

● パリのラナンキュラス (Ranunculus in Paris)
□写真 (PHOTO) P10　□材料 (MATERIAL) P56

花弁(A) 5枚
Petal(A) 5Pieces

花弁(B) 5枚
Petal(B) 5Pieces

Petal(D) 5Pieces
花弁(D) 5枚

がく
Sepal

花弁(C) 5枚
Petal(C) 5Pieces

花弁(E) 10枚
Petal(E) 10Pieces
#28 1/4 ワイヤー

葉 3枚
Leaf 3Pieces

花弁(F) 10枚
Petal(F) 10Pieces
#28 1/4 ワイヤー

● シルキーのゆり (Lily)　□写真 (PHOTO) P12　□材料 (MATERIAL) P59

12cm

花弁(小) 6枚
Petal(S) 6Pieces

花弁(大) 6枚
Petal(L) 6Pieces

72mm

葉 6枚
Leaf 6Pieces

#24白地巻きワイヤー

・77

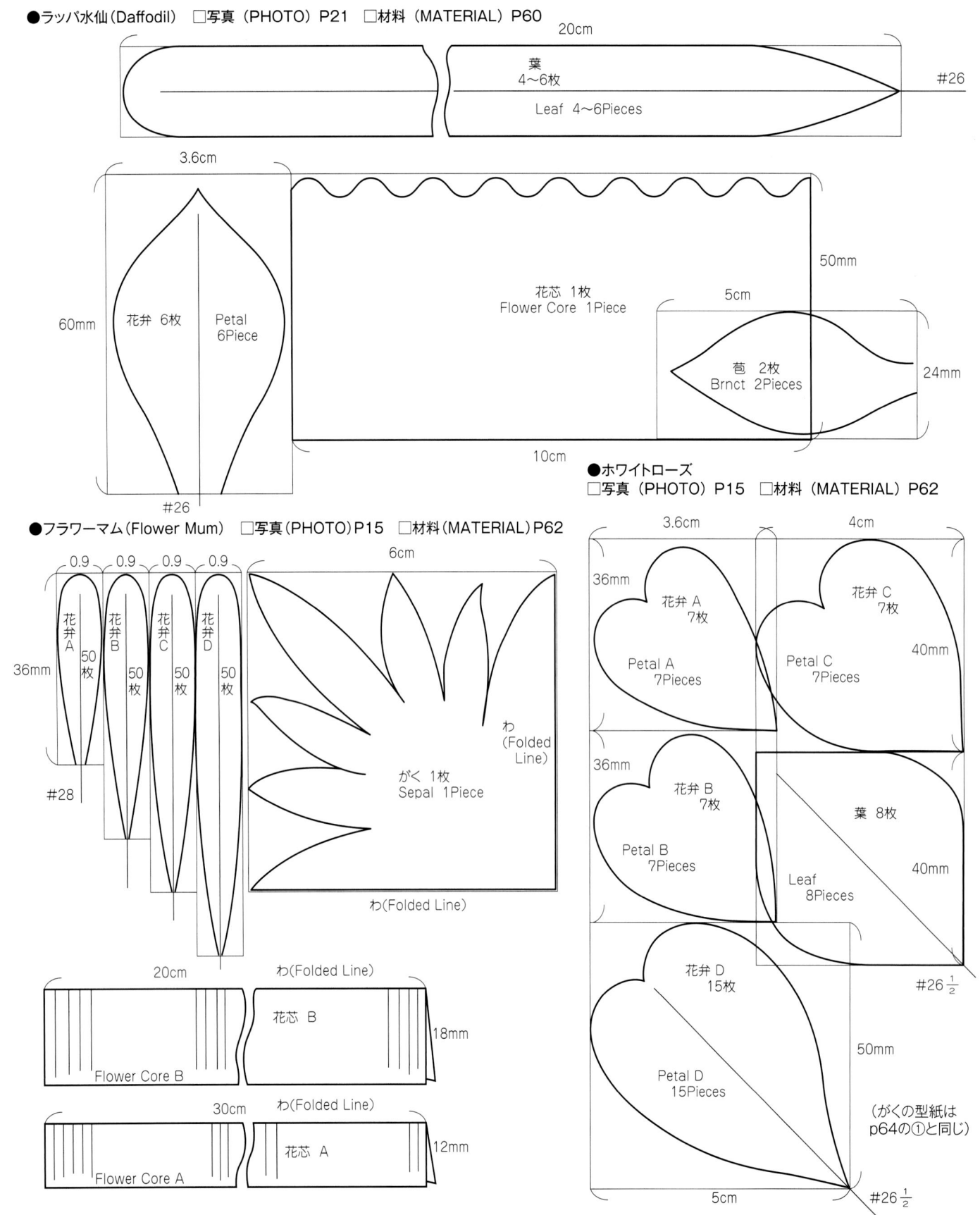

型紙　PATTERN

● ラッパ水仙 (Daffodil)　□写真（PHOTO）P21　□材料（MATERIAL）P60

20cm
葉 4～6枚
Leaf 4～6Pieces
#26

3.6cm
花弁 6枚
Petal 6Piece
60mm
#26

花芯 1枚
Flower Core 1Piece
50mm
10cm

5cm
苞 2枚
Brnct 2Pieces
24mm

● フラワーマム (Flower Mum)　■写真（PHOTO）P15　■材料（MATERIAL）P62

0.9　0.9　0.9　0.9
花弁A 50枚
花弁B 50枚
花弁C 50枚
花弁D 50枚
36mm
#28

6cm
がく 1枚
Sepal 1Piece
わ(Folded Line)
わ(Folded Line)

20cm　わ(Folded Line)
花芯 B
Flower Core B
18mm

30cm　わ(Folded Line)
花芯 A
Flower Core A
12mm

● ホワイトローズ
□写真（PHOTO）P15　□材料（MATERIAL）P62

3.6cm
花弁 A 7枚
Petal A 7Pieces
36mm

4cm
花弁 C 7枚
Petal C 7Pieces
40mm

36mm
花弁 B 7枚
Petal B 7Pieces

葉 8枚
Leaf 8Pieces
40mm
#26 1/2

5cm
花弁 D 15枚
Petal D 15Pieces
50mm

（がくの型紙は
p64の①と同じ）

#26 1/2

78・

●ミステリーローズ(Mystery-Rose)
□写真（PHOTO）P29　□材料（MATERIAL）P57

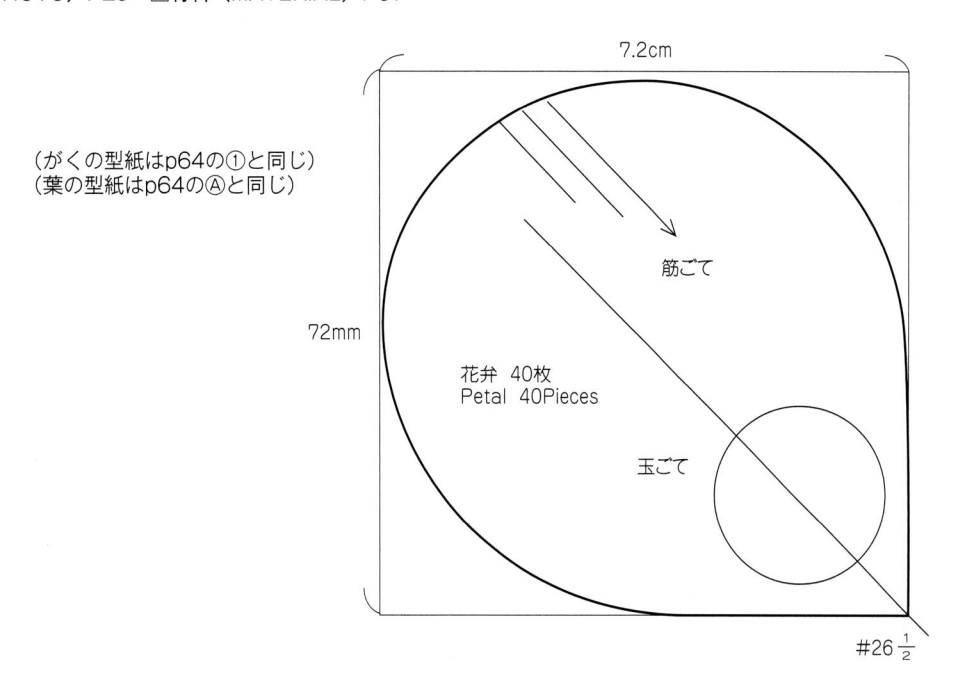

（がくの型紙はp64の①と同じ）
（葉の型紙はp64のⒶと同じ）

7.2cm
72mm
筋ごて
花弁 40枚
Petal 40Pieces
玉ごて
#26 1/2

●シルキーサンダーソニア(Silky)　□写真（PHOTO）P12　□材料（MATERIAL）P59

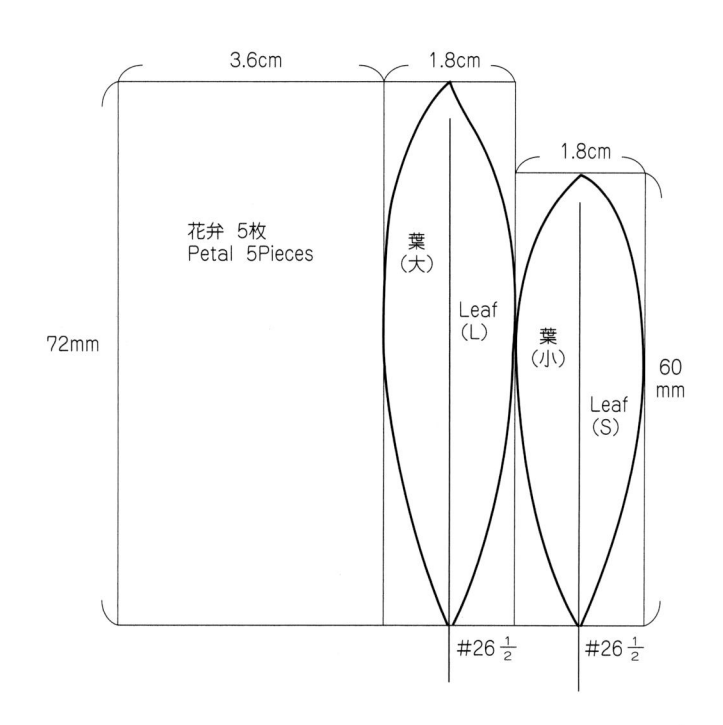

3.6cm
1.8cm
1.8cm
花弁 5枚
Petal 5Pieces
葉（大）
Leaf (L)
葉（小）
Leaf (S)
72mm
60mm
#26 1/2　#26 1/2

●著者紹介

長谷良子（はせ・よしこ）

アートディレクター・アトリエ「まじょ」主宰
ギフトラッピング・アートアカデミー理事長
ラッピングおよびリボンアートの著書多数

AOYAMA RIBBON

協力／株式会社 青山
本社／〒460-0008　愛知県名古屋市中区栄 3-10-34　☎ 052-242-1141
東京店／〒111-0052　東京都台東区柳橋 1-22-2　☎ 03-3864-1141

PHOTOGRAPHER：伊藤光雪

DTP：ティー・エー・ティー
トレス：高橋敦子

長谷良子リボンアート
リボンで花のクラフトワーク　　NDC 594.6

2012年9月30日　発　行

著　者　長谷良子
発行者　小川　雄一
発行所　株式会社誠文堂新光社
　　　　〒113-0033　東京都文京区本郷3-3-11
　　　　（編集）電話 03-5800-3616
　　　　（販売）電話 03-5800-5780
　　　　http://www.seibundo-shinkosha.net/
印刷・製本　図書印刷株式会社

© 2012, Yoshiko Hase　　　　　　　　　　　Printed in Japan
検印省略
万一乱丁・落丁本の場合はお取り換えいたします。
本書掲載記事の無断転用を禁じます。

本書のコピー、スキャン、デジタル化等の無断複製は著作権法上での例外を除き禁じられています。本書を代行業者等の第三者に依頼してスキャンやデジタル化することは、たとえ個人や家庭内での利用であっても著作権法上認められません。

Ⓡ〈日本複製権センター委託出版物〉
本書の全部または一部を無断で複写複製（コピー）することは、著作権法上での例外を除き禁じられています。本書からの複写を希望される場合は日本複製権センター（JRRC）の許諾を受けてください。
JRRC（http://www.jrrc.or.jp/）E-Mail:jrrc_info@jrrc.or.jo　電話 03-3401-2382）

ISBN978-4-416-91266-9

リボンアートへのお誘い
●下記教室へお問い合わせ下さい

長谷　恵	☎ 045-892-1743
中村千鶴子	☎ 095-838-3259
宮原美代子	☎ 092-943-5227
余村則子	☎ 048-644-1678
石鍋綾野	☎ 03-3990-0815
後藤幸子	☎ 0587-81-8614
平瀬恵子	☎ 0790-63-0559
角田憲子	☎ 0798-65-0030
田中陽子	☎ 0875-72-4121
村田里美	☎ 0299-78-3230
有松光子	☎ 0978-63-5871
相澤美栄子	☎ 045-361-3841
木村紅美	☎ 089-923-9393
大野日出子	☎ 072-762-4871
柏原純子	☎ 011-782-6424
太田さつき	☎ 0564-43-2016
西山博美	☎ 0736-25-0092
木村智代	☎ 0569-29-0018
上田洋子	☎ 0297-66-8067
藤森浩子	☎ 03-3612-8924
橘内美彌	☎ 015-324-2884
中川雅子	☎ 011-572-2295
嶋田和江	☎ 042-955-6041
浅野愛子	☎ 052-321-7412
周麗瑛	（台湾）
陳文英	（台湾）
浅山啓子	☎ 0727-83-3383
梶本由喜代	☎ 0734-71-9068
杉山恭子	☎ 052-895-4672
本間洋子	☎ 03-5605-9154
前川美佐子	☎ 0795-52-2403
諸角和子	☎ 0489-42-1666
佐伯馨子	☎ 047-465-3565
原　美那子	☎ 0573-25-5671
伊藤佳子	☎ 052-806-8861
畑 はづき	☎ 0567-95-3252
時安雪子	☎ 0725-43-4699
桝屋ミサオ	☎ 0834-31-7129
十田幾代	☎ 03-3442-7168
加藤規子	☎ 052-739-7687
福田一枝	☎ 0489-75-0374
松崎美奈子	☎ 0569-34-3435
岡本弘子	☎ 0566-42-9133
板倉佐喜子	☎ 0565-28-0869
長坂裕見子	☎ 0564-32-0495
末松朱美	☎ 097-535-1895
金仙英	（韓国）
杉野智子	☎ 0978-33-4668
小木曽敦子	☎ 052-700-3891
梁雅惠	（台湾）
橋本明美	☎ 0476-46-1069
羅景霞	（台湾）
古村和左子	☎ 0745-72-2833
土屋紀子	☎ 076-243-1526
村上れい子	☎ 076-433-7044
草 直美	☎ 0766-61-2598
金姓垠	（韓国）
崔順玉	（韓国）
西谷典子	☎ 0155-34-6777